MILLIONAIRE WITHIN

PRAISE FOR MILLIONAIRE WITHIN

"Wow, you can't make this stuff up. A raw and uncut rollercoaster ride that will leave you thoroughly entertained and enlightened. This book is like being a fly on the wall witnessing the bold power moves and persistence necessary on your journey towards financial freedom. Buckle up and prepare to be shocked and inspired."

- Ron Douglas
New York Times Best Seller

"These stories are both entertaining and educating. Each chapter plays out like the script of a movie. E. Brian Rose reveals secrets of our business that are found nowhere else.

- Daven Michaels
New York Times Best Seller

"Engaging... Intriguing... E. Brian Rose is masterful at mixing stories with teaching concepts. This book reads like a Hollywood movie!"

-James Malinchak
Featured on ABCs Hit TV Show, "Secret Millionaire"
Author of the Top-Selling Book, *Millionaire Success Secrets*
Founder, BigMoneySpeaker.com

"'*Millionaire Within*' is a book every entrepreneur needs to read. E. Brian Rose does a fantastic job taking you through the 'real' world of business building. And of course all roads lead to the Internet. You either understand online marketing or you are walking dead, but just don't know it yet."

-Wayne Allyn Root
Bestselling author of "*The Power of RELENTLESS*"
Former Vice Presidential nominee & National Media Personality
Founder of WayneRoot.com, RelentlessROOT.com, ROOTforAmerica.com
and WinningEDGE.com

"Real, relevant, and spot on! E. Brian Rose shares a powerful story of struggle, setbacks and ultimate success that keeps the reader engage page by page. A must read for any budding online entrepreneur."

- Brian G. Johnson
Author, Speaker, Poodle Wrangler
MarketingEasyStreet.com

"I read this book cover to cover in one sitting. As a parable of perseverance in pursuit of profit and passion, this book is hard to beat."

- Colin Theriot

World Renowned Copywriter

Maximus of the Cult of Copy

"E. Brian Rose shares in tremendous and often hilarious detail about how you can follow his lead to successfully traverse this sometimes seemingly impossible & never ending course to truly and finally awaken your *Millionaire Within*. Go for it! I dare you."

- Tom Beal

Founder of MakeTodayGreat.com

MILLIONAIRE WITHIN

Untold Stories from the Internet Underworld

E. BRIAN ROSE

NEW YORK

Millionaire Within
Untold Stories from the Internet Underworld

© 2016 E. Brian Rose

I have tried to recreate events, locales and conversations from my memories of them. In order to maintain their anonymity, in some instances I have changed the names of individuals and places. I may have changed some identifying characteristics and details, such as physical properties, occupations, and places of residence.

Published in New York, New York, by Morgan James Publishing. Morgan James and The Entrepreneurial Publisher are trademarks of Morgan James, LLC. www.MorganJamesPublishing.com

The Morgan James Speakers Group can bring authors to your live event. For more information or to book an event visit The Morgan James Speakers Group at www.TheMorganJamesSpeakersGroup.com.

A **free** eBook edition is available with the purchase of this print book.

ISBN 9781630473457   paperback
ISBN 9781630473464   eBook
ISBN 9781630473471   hardcover
Library of Congress Control Number: 2014944218

CLEARLY PRINT YOUR NAME ABOVE IN UPPER CASE

Instructions to claim your free eBook edition:
1. Download the BitLit app for Android or iOS
2. Write your name in **UPPER CASE** on the line
3. Use the BitLit app to submit a photo
4. Download your eBook to any device

Cover Design by:
Rachel Lopez
www.r2cdesign.com

Interior Design by:
Chris Treccani
www.3dogdesign.net

In an effort to support local communities, raise awareness and funds, Morgan James Publishing donates a percentage of all book sales for the life of each book to Habitat for Humanity Peninsula and Greater Williamsburg.

Get involved today, visit
www.MorganJamesBuilds.com

Habitat
for Humanity®
Peninsula and
Greater Williamsburg
Building Partner

DEDICATION

*To Madeleine and Justin, my beautiful children
and future entrepreneurs.*

TABLE OF CONTENTS

ACKNOWLEDGMENTS

I thought about writing this book for some time, but kept putting it off. It was the pushing of Rich Wilens that led me to start banging on the keyboard for a few hours a day.

There were many people who helped me make the stories of this book a reality, a couple had no idea they were even a factor, but I would like to thank them, anyway. Those people are Dr. Mark Kerble (the only teacher that ever saw any potential in me) and Henry "Butchy" Lucas (my childhood friend's father who first taught me the phrase "work hard, play hard").

I am where I am today thanks to the friendship, partnership, and motivation of James J. Jones, Herb Van Dyke, Bryan Zimmerman, Chad Casselman, Mike Carraway, Brad Gosse, Justin Quick, Ron Douglas, Bill Guthrie, Colin Theriot, Gerald Glynn, Bob Van Court, Dr. Ben Adkins, Ben Littlefield, Anthony Aires, Brad Spencer, Dan Ardebili, Mike Cowles, David Eisner, Michael Haynes, Mike Chauvin, Mike Lantz, Sam England, Brian McLeod, and to the many other partners and friends that have stood by me, along the way.

FOREWORD

The year was 1995, and the Internet was the new frontier. Like the 19th century wild west, the first Internet gold rush saw unprecedented venture capital poured into anything with a dotcom at the end of its name. And like the early settlers, there were fortunes made... and lost.

There were only 18,000 websites in the entire world in 1995, and I was fortunate enough to have created one of them. While I have enjoyed great success on the Internet, my version of the wild west was like a John Wayne film. The bad guy done someone wrong, the damsel in distress needed rescuin', and at The Duke's command a posse was sent out to procure justice. Like these early Hollywood versions of the west, there were casualties, but not a lot of blood.

The same can't be said of E. Brian Rose. His Internet and entrepreneurial exploits play out more like Clint Eastwood's film, Unforgiven. Gritty. Raw. Casualties. This is the Internet Wild, Wild West portrayed as a real-life gold rush with larger-than-life characters, of which "EBR" has earned the right to tell.

From the warn-torn battlefields of Somalia to the relationship-scarred partnership feuds of the Internet, E. Brian Rose has been on the front lines as a participant, and a witness, to people, places and incidents that sound like they were scripted for a Hollywood film. But they weren't. This the true story of a man who saw gold in them thar hills, and grabbed his pick, trusty six-shooter, modem, mouse and keyboard to chisel out a place in Internet history.

From software and ebay to private placements and creating a powerhouse of an affiliate network, EBR spins story after story of interesting characters (punctuated by his own "colorful" style of story-telling).

So saddle up, cowboys and cowgirls. Gather 'round the campfire and listen up as Uncle Brian shares the good, the bad and the ugly of the online world. It's inspiring and enlightening, but it t'aint always purty.

One thing is for sure. It's all real, but the good guy isn't about to ride off into the sunset. While he's covered a lot of ground already, you be sure that this is just the beginning for E. Brian Rose.

Set a spell with Brian, and remember that if you ask Mr. Taggart for a can of beans, likely he'll tell you that you've had enough.

- Joel Comm
New York Times Best Selling Author

Entrepreneurship is a journey. It's a mindset, a lifestyle, and an adventure.

It is a never ending course of learning that no school on earth could possibly teach. You must live it to understand it.

You must be willing to take a leap down a rabbit hole that leads to a place where everything goes against what the average person believes.

Once inside, you will experience disappointment, failure, and sometimes even disaster. However, it is a path you must be willing to take if you truly want to experience independence and absolute freedom.

CHAPTER 1

TWENTY IS TOO MUCH, MON

I was half asleep, half thinking about what it would be like when we landed. There was a muffled bang.

The loadmaster gets on the PA system and tells everybody to get buckled.

Then, in mid speech, he drops the microphone and runs to his seat.

The world's largest cargo plane started to waiver from side to side. An army colonel sitting next to me whispers, "I'm pretty sure this is it." Disregarding our major difference in rank, I whisper back, "Shut the fuck up, sir!"

Hours earlier, we took off from a makeshift airstrip, somewhere in the Egyptian desert. The fire bottle in one of the engines went out and we were forced to make an emergency landing. For three days, we waited for a maintenance crew to arrive. There was a single large tent with sour orange juice, Twizzlers, a TV and VCR. The movie *Candy Man* played on a loop the entire time.

Flames were now shooting from one of the engines. Apparently, the fire bottle, whatever that is, wasn't fixed correctly. We were going down. At a 45 degree angle, I could see green grass through my window. It was getting closer.

The next minute of my life is a blur. Zero recollection. All I know is we made it.

I spent the rest of the week at a German beach resort in Mombasa, Kenya. On a walk through some bad neighborhoods, I overheard a business deal going down. "Twenty is too much, mon," said one guy. The other countered by saying he would throw in a small bag of weed. "Done," the first man said. The next day, I saw him selling the two dozen wooden figurines for fifteen dollars each. All 24 of them were sold to tourists before lunch.

Back on a plane. This time, a smaller C141 jet would be taking us to our final destination. As we approached the airport, an announcement was made saying the landing strip was hot and the plane would not be stopping. We were told to jump out and run straight ahead, towards the cafeteria.

I was one of the last to deplane. I stumbled a bit while stepping off the still moving aircraft. As I regained balance, I could hear heavy machine gun fire all around. I stopped to look around. "Are you stupid? Run means run, asshole." I don't know who said it, but it was clear he was yelling at me.

In the cafeteria, we laid down next to rows of neatly stacked sandbags. *CNN International* was playing on a big screen TV. Coincidentally, the story was about Mogadishu, Somalia. We laughed as the woman reported there has been no hostility in almost two weeks.

It had been twelve days since Bloody Monday, the day two U.S. Blackhawks were shot down. The incident was later retold in the movie *Blackhawk Down*. My team was there to document what was going on. I was part of a joint Combat Camera unit made up of combat photographers and video producers from the Army, Marines, and Air Force. We were part soldier, part journalist.

During my time in "The Dish," I would link up with various units making their rounds throughout the theater. From kicking in doors on weapon searches to a local medicine man tarring and feathering a young kid who was injured playing with a grenade, I videotaped it all, while practicing the fine art of knowing when to put the camera down and when to pick the rifle up.

A couple of months into the deployment, one of the major TV networks realized it was the one-year anniversary of Marine forces storming the beaches and they wanted to put together a last-minute special. Word got out to journalists in the region that the networks were seeking any and all footage from the previous twelve months. I tell my commander that we could make a fortune. He laughs, as if I were joking.

It was around midnight when an independent producer from South Africa knocked on the door of our makeshift video editing suite. He said he acquired permission via the Freedom of Information Act to make copies of all our unclassified footage. I was told to gather tapes for him and make the dupes.

The next day, he tells me he sold twenty of the 90 minutes of our footage at a thousand dollars a minute. Being in the military and seeing all the business that goes on around the military is painful to an entrepreneur. It's like watching the world pass you by.

From the beaches of Kenya to the battlefields of Somalia, business was happening all around me and I was inspired. People were getting rich, oftentimes by taking advantage of other people's work. I took mental notes and I was ready. Ready to go home. Ready to make my mark. Ready to make my millions.

CHAPTER 2

SPAM

I got a call from Matt, a kid from the old neighborhood in Boston. He had just graduated from broadcasting school and wanted to talk about starting a production company.

The timing was perfect for me. I was freshly out of the military, had a ton of real world experience, and looking to start making some real dough. The only problem was money. Both of us were broke and we would need to buy some production equipment. Matt suggested we talk to his dad about a loan, so I flew back home for the meeting. His dad agreed to lend us $5,000 and accept interest only payments for the first year. This was enough to get us a quality camera and a couple of editing decks. We jumped in Matt's car and made the trip from Boston to Biloxi in less than 26 hours.

Matt was a year younger than me and never had a girlfriend. In our high school years, he was always a third wheel, often whining that he was bored while everybody else was paired up and making out. After high school, he became obsessed with Billy Joel. OK, everybody loves the Piano Man, but when he came down to live with me, he hung a poster of the guy above his bed. Quite strange for a twenty one year old.

I was working the seven to midnight shift at Kicker 108, our small market country music radio station. I hosted a show called "Cryin, Lovin, Laughin, or Leavin". Tweens and young teens would light up my phones all night, so they could share their problems and express their never dying love for each other. Small market radio didn't pay much. I took home about a thousand dollars a month.

During the day, I was working on generating leads for our new company. We called it Ace Video Productions. Biloxi is a casino town, so the name was fitting, but the real reason we chose it was to show up first in the Yellow Pages.

My girlfriend was a massage therapist at a chiropractic clinic. She set me up a meeting with Dr. Cleveland and I explained what the company could do for his business. The next day, Ace Video Productions had its first gig producing a video about back rehabilitation.

As the weeks went by, the phone rang more and more. It was not steady work, but these small jobs were paying the bills.

I came home from the radio station one night to find Matt sitting in front of a new computer. I was pretty pissed that he would spend the last of his dad's loan money towards something so expensive, without first consulting me.

The computer box sitting on the floor was about two feet tall and almost fifty pounds. The weight of the bulky monitor made my flimsy kitchen table top bend. There was a phone line attached to the back, allowing us to dial in to America Online. AOL was the shit. You could read the news and search through the members directory for local girls to stalk.

I went to work that night and gave my email address out to my listeners. I felt so cool, as I was one of the first people in my circle to have an electronic mail account. When I got home, I had three emails waiting for me. The wheels were spinning. There had to be a way to make money from this.

On a trip to Office Depot, I was browsing the software aisle. Actually, it was just a section of an aisle, as there weren't that many titles to choose from back then. I spotted a package that made these cool looking printouts about the day you were born. You type in the date and it spits out a framable document. It was ten bucks, so I bought it.

AOL had a section where you could place free classified ads. I figured I could take a shot at selling these birthday history thingamajigees.

First week: two sales.

I didn't have a way to collect payments online, so I had the buyers send me a check for five dollars. I had already made my investment back. All future sales would be pure profit.

Two sales in a week were impressive for such a cheesy product, but it was not enough for me. I decided to get a little aggressive. I went through the AOL member directory and started pasting copies of the ad in emails to the members. Later, this practice would become known as spam, but back then it was cool to get email and people were very responsive.

I sold about fifty, before AOL shut down our account. Apparently, a few people got angry and reported me. I guess some people didn't think getting email was as cool as I did.

Oh well, at least I still had the production company. Or so I thought.

I came home from work one night to find the house almost empty. Matt had packed up everything and headed home. The camera, the editing deck, the computer, it was all gone.

A week later, I was fired from the radio station and was forced to move. I ended up renting a thirty year old house on wheels in a trashy trailer park.

It was time to start looking for a real job.

CHAPTER 3

TRAINING ON TAX PAYER'S DIME

After a series of dead end jobs, in 1998, I landed a job working at Stennis Space Center as a video producer for the Naval Oceanographic Office. It was a cushy job that paid very well. For the first time in my life, I was making over $70,000 a year, but it was killing me. It turns out working for the government may be the fastest ticket to boredom and depression.

The position was vacant for a few months before I started. During that time, the folks in charge decided to purchase a new editing system. Without the guidance of an experienced video guy, they relied on a salesman to tell them what they needed. The result was a million dollar system that was about ten years outdated.

When I started, they were excited to show me their new purchase. I informed them the system they had was a dinosaur and the rest of the world was in the non-linear age. I expected disappointment, but they smiled and said, "Just buy whatever system you want." I went on to replace their million dollar fiasco with an updated $7,000 digital system.

A few weeks later, I was asked to make a list and purchase any software I may need. I spent about $300 buying various editing tools. They came back to me and said that wasn't enough, "We'll need you to spend a bunch more on software." It didn't matter to them whether or not I actually had a use for the software. That was the budget and they needed the money spent.

Years later, it occurred to me how corrupt these government "spend it or lose it" budgets can be. Imagine if I had a friend in the software business. I could have bought everything from him. Or I could have signed up for affiliate deals for mainstream software and took a kickback from every purchase made.

I mentioned this job was killing me. It wasn't all the hard work that was doing me in. My problem was sheer boredom. My day consisted of a ten minute morning meeting, a two hour lunch, then wait to go home at five.

Six months into my time at the space center, I was assigned my first major project. It was a fifteen minute overview video that was to be shown to politicians and other VIPs touring the facility. They told me the project had a short deadline, so I would have to work hard to bust it out on time. This was no problem for me, as I came from the fast paced world of the producing the news for the military and there was always a short deadline. After seeing what they wanted done, in my head, I estimated it would take about two weeks to write the script, shoot the necessary footage, and edit the final product.

"How long do I have?"

"We need it by July 15th."

"July? Are you sure?"

"Why, do you need more time?"

It was December.

The final video had an old time marine feel to it. Originally, I did the voiceover myself, but I felt my voice was a bit too young for this, so I called Terry, a buddy of mine from my radio days. He had a much older, raspier voice. It would be perfect for the production.

Terry said he would do the audio work for $300. I emailed him the script and he sent me a CD the next day. My bosses thought he sounded great, but they balked at the fee. They said, "It would look fishy if we paid him just $300. We need to pay him the going SAG rates."

I called Terry to explain that we were unable to pay what he was asking. He couldn't believe the government was unable to afford $300. I said, "Terry, they refuse to pay you $300, but they are sending a check for $1,200." Terry didn't complain anymore.

For the next year, I spent most of my time surfing the Internet. The world was changing fast and the Internet was exploding. I watched from my cubicle as idiots got funded millions of dollars for dumb ideas that probably wouldn't ever make a dime.

I decided I was going to start using my time at "work" to throw my hat into the dot com arena. I knew nothing about creating websites, but I had all the time in the world to learn.

CHAPTER 4

DOT COM DREAMS

A friend hooked me up with some software that made building sites a snap. I started learning about affiliate programs. An affiliate program is where you send people to a website and get paid a commission if they make a purchase. My first shot at it was a website called Go Biloxi. I signed up as an affiliate for one of the few travel sites out there and made a commission each time somebody booked a hotel room in Biloxi, MS.

I started listing the link in all of the directories. Back then, I had no idea this was called backlinking and, apparently, the search engines dig that stuff. Then, something crazy happened. My site got ranked really well in Yahoo. The people started coming - and they were booking hotel rooms! Things were much different back them. A few good keywords, a bunch of content, and some backlinks was all it took to get high search engine rankings, even in a lucrative niche, such as travel. As the Internet grew, this would become harder and harder to achieve.

I followed this up by creating identical sites for other cities. It was like using a cookie cutter. All I had to do was change the name of the site and the location of what hotels I wanted to appear. I wasn't making the big bucks, but a couple of hundred bucks a week was nothing to sneeze at, especially since it was a 'set it and forget it" type of system. I did the work one time and the sites continued to pay.

I thought I could make even more money by selling similar travel websites to others wanting to get in the game. I listed a brand new site on eBay and it quickly sold for $900. Soon, I was creating and selling these sites at the pace of five a week. This practice would later become known as "site flipping", but at the time, I seemed to be the only one doing it.

Unfortunately, this was only lucrative for a few months. It wasn't long before more and more people started selling their cookie-cutter websites on eBay. Along with the rush of new sites, came a race to the bottom. Pretty soon, quality looking websites were being sold for under ten dollars. It was no longer worth my time to flip sites, but it was a heck of a run, with very little effort, so I wasn't complaining too much.

One of the people that bought a site from me was George, a former IRS agent running a tax prep service in Tujunga, California. George called me and we talked for hours about some of his own dot com dreams.

I remember thinking how interesting this man sounded. He was born in Lebanon and grew up in Kuwait. If I recall correctly, his mother was Greek. His accent was pretty cool.

We kept in touch for the next few weeks. Each time we talked, George would give more details about his vision. We shared similar visions, although mine were just pipedreams at the time. Impressed by my limited web design talents, George offered to fly me out to California and help him create some website templates. He was also going to pay me handsomely. I put in for some vacation time and went.

Tujunga is a decent sized town, about an hour outside of L.A. George's office was quite impressive. He leased a large building in the downtown area. Inside, he had a fairly large staff of employees. Some were managing the office and clients; others seemed to be just there to serve George. There was an old man, probably in his seventies, that would do anything George asked, from getting him a cup of coffee to pulling weeds in his front lawn.

I spent a week with George and his fiancée, Yvonne. During that time, we talked about how he wanted to raise millions of dollars for an Internet business. I didn't know if it was his being so close to Silicon Valley or the hourly glasses of scotch that made him think he could raise that kind of money, but it sounded sexy, so I listened.

George's dream was to challenge eBay. He was convinced he could raise enough money from private investors to take on one of the world's biggest websites. While I never imagined he would come close to achieving that goal, I thought even if he could grab a small percentage of the online auction market, that would be a pretty decent chunk of change.

On the last day of my visit, George was supposed to pay me $5,000 for my work. Just hours before he was going to drive me back to LAX airport, he posed an offer to me. I could take the check for five grand or I could drive home in one of his three vintage cars. I chose the latter and three days later, pulled into my Biloxi, MS driveway in a near mint condition 1973 candy apple red convertible Corvette.

The car made me think exactly what George wanted me to think. He was the real deal.

A few weeks later, he made me an offer to work for him full time. This was a hard decision, as I had a job making seventy thousand a year and it was one of those jobs where it would take an act of Congress to lose. But the Internet was the future and I knew I would never make millions working for the government.

George offered me $60,000 a year and two million shares of stock in the newly created "BidBay.com". I took the deal and quit my job.

BidBay.com kicked off like gangbusters. George put a fund raising team together that included a former U.S. Congressman and some fancy Wall Street guys. The money started to pour in. Millions, just as he said it would. The official launch of the site came after a professionally produced TV commercial aired during the NFL playoffs. I remember sitting in George's living room hitting the refresh button to see how many people signed up. Thousands were coming in every minute. This was going to be big.

I was flying back and forth between Mississippi and LA about twice a month. I liked working from home, but my time in Tujunga made me feel like royalty. Every lunch was catered and every day ended with beer and scotch. Dinners were at the finest restaurants in town. This was the life I wanted to live.

Once, towards the end of a strategy meeting, a woman walked in and arrogantly said she needed to paint George's building. She was a location manager for a major production company. A few weeks later, I was back in town and on the set of a John Travolta movie. Things were great.

Then a speed bump.

George called one morning and told me the company was being sued by eBay for using the word "Bay" in the name. After a short battle, BidBay gave up and turned the trademark and domain name over. But that didn't stop George. After some regrouping and under a new name of AuctionDiner, the company went forward, raising even more millions.

The money was coming from a private placement memorandum, or PPM. A team of fast talking, market savvy telemarketers were calling private investors and telling them of the great potential the site had. This was 1999 and money was flowing all over the dot com world, so I never thought twice about it. There was talk of an IPO and I was holding a ton of shares. I was going to be rich. Life was good.

Then it wasn't.

Almost four months into my employment and despite a one year employment contract, George called to tell me I was fired. I couldn't believe it. The company implemented just about every marketing idea I threw out there and the site was growing rapidly. This was absurd. He even wanted my stock back, saying I didn't finish the required one year of employment in order to keep the shares. I was pissed, but wasn't going down without a fight.

I did what every good Jewish boy from Boston would do. I lawyered up and filed suit.

George had an insurance policy that covered lawsuits like these and the case was quickly settled. As I recall, the settlement was around a hundred thousand dollars. Of course, the lawyers got a good chunk of that, but a fair share still went into my pocket. I also got a good bit of the stock back. There was still hope for me to make millions off of this online auction site. I paid close attention to what the company was doing, in hopes of hearing those three wonderful letters: IPO.

Months later, George and I made amends. Despite the fact that he tried to screw me, I missed the guy. He was like a cartoon character, full of life and very spontaneous. He asked me to once again work for him and come up with a redesign for the site. I flew out to meet with him and Yvonne at their new house - a hillside mansion, complete with tennis courts and Arabian horses. Call me crazy, but I took the job. No contract this time, just a project that took about three months to complete and paid a pretty good penny.

In 2000, the dot com bubble had burst. The chances of an IPO were now slim to none. George and I spoke less and less, but I still kept my ears open. I was a shareholder and I still had hope that I would make my fortune with this company.

Years later, I got a call from George. Once again, he wanted to hire me. By this time, I was living in Las Vegas and well into the next chapter of my life. But Tujunga was just a few hours away, so I made the drive in to hear what ol' Georgie had to say.

He was looking for a new direction. eBay was stronger than ever and many smaller online auction sites failed at taking on the giant. BidBay / AuctionDiner was one of them.

This was right around the time when social media was sprouting up. MySpace was in its heyday and people were starting to talk about a site called FaceBook. My idea for George was to socialize the site. Make it more of a community where buyers and sellers could interact. Turn it into the "MySpace of auction sites".

George loved the idea and offered me a good deal of money to handle the redesign. I took the deal, but this time, I outsourced all the work. George and his team loved the final product. They relaunched the site under the new name of AuctionCities. This was an idea that I believed could work. I had new hope for that stock certificate collecting dust in my file cabinet.

Again, the months went by and George and I talked less and less. The site and George were almost out of my mind completely, when I caught an article online saying he was being sued for fraud.

All those millions the company was raking in, the mansion on the hill… well, apparently, things weren't on the up and up. He was sued by investors, who claimed they were lied to. I read about some investors being told the company was on the verge of being bought by eBay. Others said they were told former President George Bush was on the board of directors. The stories got more and more farfetched. In the end, George and company lost and so went his money, the company, and my hopes of ever cashing in.

It has been about seven years since I spoke to George. When I started writing this book, I decided it was time I give him a call. I was planning to catch up on some old stories and make sure I was accurate in my retelling of them.

The number I had for George was his private cell phone number. He had the same number for many years, so I was surprised to hear the disconnected recording when I called. Looking for a new number,

I Googled him. I could not believe what I found. Wait. That's not entirely true. I certainly did believe it and wasn't at all surprised.

George was behind bars.

It seems the former IRS agent was busted by current IRS agents. SEC investigators, too.

According to prosecutors, George did not disclose to investors that half their money was going to telemarketers as commission. Another portion was, apparently, going directly to George; nearly $3 million of it. That money was not reported as income.

George pleaded guilty to charges of conspiracy and filing a false tax return. He was sentenced to almost three years in federal prison and ordered to pay back $8.8 million to 216 investors.

As for the Corvette George gave me – ironically, I ended up selling it on eBay, of all places. I used the money for a down payment on a new house.

I still have that stock certificate.

CHAPTER 5

MY FIRST MEDIA FRENZY

While working with George, I developed a good relationship with the third party software developer that created the auction engine for BidBay. After George and I split and prior to the settlement, I decided to use the same technology and take a shot at starting my own auction site. I created the design and called it "DutchBid".

I didn't have any money to promote the new site, so I had to think outside the box. The timing was actually perfect. While vegging out on the couch, I came across a very interesting news story about Kevin Mitnick, the man known as the first hacker to be jailed for his hacking crimes in the United States.

Here's what Wikipedia has to say about him:

> *In 1979, he broke into his first computer. He was sentenced to 12 months in prison followed by three years of supervised release. Near the end of his supervised release, Mitnick hacked into Pacific Bell*

21

voice mail computers. After a warrant was issued for his arrest, Mitnick fled, becoming a fugitive for two and a half years.

According to the U.S. Department of Justice, Mitnick gained unauthorized access to dozens of computer networks while he was a fugitive. He used cloned cellular phones to hide his location and, among other things, copied valuable proprietary software from some of the country's largest cellular telephone and computer companies. Mitnick also intercepted and stole computer passwords, altered computer networks, and broke into and read private e-mail. Mitnick was apprehended on February 15, 1995 in Raleigh, North Carolina. He was found with cloned cellular phones, more than 100 clone cellular phone codes, and multiple pieces of false identification.

Mitnick served five years in prison — four and a half years pre-trial and eight months in solitary confinement — because, according to Mitnick, law enforcement officials convinced a judge that he had the ability to "start a nuclear war by whistling into a pay phone", meaning that law enforcement told the judge that he could somehow dial into the NORAD modem via a payphone from prison and communicate with the modem by whistling to launch nuclear missiles.

He was released on January 21, 2000. In December of that year, Mitnick tried to raise some funds by selling a variety of items on eBay. He listed one of his cell phones, a small computer, and two of his prison identification cards. eBay decided they did not want the business of a hacker and closed the auctions. He then went to Amazon and Yahoo. Both had auction sites at the time and both gave Mitnick the same treatment. Mitnick was somewhat of a celebrity in geek world, so it was no surprise the media grabbed a hold of this story.

This was my opportunity!

It didn't take much searching to find a telephone number for Mitnick. I called him and offered DutchBid as a venue to run his auctions. His first concern was there was relatively no traffic at the site and barely fifty auction listings. I assured him that would not be the case, once he listed his items. In reality, I had no idea if the press would still be interested, but I painted a picture of the media swarming to cover the auctions. It worked.

As a part of his release, the judge ordered that Mitnick could not touch a computer for five years, so all my future email communications were between Mitnick's father and me (ya right). His "father" set up an account on DutchBid and listed the items. In addition to the items previously taken down by eBay, Mitnick listed several autographed bumper stickers with the slogan "Free Kevin", which was the battle cry of fellow hackers during Mitnick's incarceration.

Immediately after the auctions were listed, I wrote a short press release that read:

> *After being shut down by eBay, Yahoo and Amazon auctions, Kevin Mitnick's genuine prison ID cards and other personal items are back on the auction block.*

This time at DutchBid.com.

On Monday, eBay had pulled the auction of Kevin Mitnick's Federal Bureau of Prisons inmate ID card, ending a flow of authentic Mitnick merchandise that was placed up for auction by Mitnick's father. Kevin Mitnick is barred from using computers and accessing the web under the terms of his supervised prison release.

Kevin Mitnick, who has been called a "computer terrorist" by the Department of Justice, is perhaps the most high-profile computer criminal to date.

The official Kevin Mitnick web site claims that, "Kevin pursued his hacking as a means of satisfying his intellectual curiosity and applying Yankee ingenuity. These attributes are more frequently promoted rather than punished by society."

DutchBid founder and president Eric B. Rosenberg feels that that Mitnick memorabilia should be available to the public. He stated, "Whether you believe that Kevin is a criminal or a hero is irrelevant. The fact that the 'big three' auction sites would remove Mitnick memorabilia, but allow the auctioning of Nazi material is absurd. Kevin Mitnick's personal items are certainly welcome at DutchBid.com."

I submitted that press release to PRweb.com and paid the small fee. Then, I did a search for all the news outlets, blogs, and opinionates that wrote about the Mitnick/eBay story online. I emailed a copy of the press release to each of the writers. After 24 hours, I was disappointed to only receive a call from one of them. It was a small online news site that I can't even remember the name of. The reporter wanted an interview with Mitnick and me. Later that day, we had a three way call. I was asked three questions and the rest of the thirty minute call was spent questioning Mitnick. A few hours later, the interview was posted online. It was no swarm, but I was happy to have just one article written about my new site.

That night, just as I was about to head off to bed, the phone rang. I thought, "Who could be calling me at two in the morning?" I almost didn't answer. "Is this DutchBid.com," said the female voice on the other line. I said yes. It was Kelly Yamanouchi, a reporter for the Associated Press, which was the biggest wire service at the time. She said she had a tight deadline, so she rushed through a few questions and quickly hung up. I went to bed.

I woke up around 9am and turned my computer on. I had over 4,000 emails! Most of them were notifications of new registrations at DutchBid, but a lot of them were from reporters wanting an interview. I opened my browser to find out where the traffic was coming from. It was from all over the world! There were news articles being published about DutchBid in every language imaginable, although most of the traffic was coming from articles published in the United States.

CNet.com wrote about my site. *USA Today, CNN, The Register, The Chicago Tribune, US News & World Reports*, and hundreds of other websites all published articles about DutchBid. Many of them are still online, just do a Google search for Kevin Mitnick and DutchBid and you'll see them.

I spent the next several hours calling back reporters and answering questions. They basically just wanted a quote from me, so I tried to change up what I said to each of them, while still giving the same answer.

By the end of the day, a bidding war for Mitnick's things was underway. It was amazing. One of his two ID cards was already in the thousands – the bidding barely reached a grand when eBay shut down their auction. Something even better was happening, too. People were listing new items on the site. In just 12 hours, over 500 new items were listed up for auction.

This was all happening shortly after I filed my lawsuit against George. In the midst of the media storm, I received an email from him. It said, "Well done, you son of a bitch. Too bad I don't have anybody working for me that was smart enough to think of this." I liked getting that email. It was his way of giving me a pat on the back, despite our turmoil.

Within a few days, over one million unique visitors had come to DutchBid. I knew these types of news stories have a short shelf life, so I started thinking about ways to keep the spotlight on the site. Clearly, many other small auction sites were taking notice. I thought this might be a chance to leverage the press I was getting and make a deal to merge with one of those companies.

After a bit of searching, I found the perfect target. It was a site that had just announced they would be shutting down. You might ask why I would be interested in a company on their way out. It was their assets. The site, called Gold's Auctions, had tens of thousands of registered users and about 100,000 items listed. That's what I was after.

I contacted the owners. Sure enough, they had seen the media frenzy surrounding DutchBid and the Mitnick auctions. They were impressed. Gold's was pulling the plug on their site, because of debts they were unable to pay. Their bad decisions spelled opportunity for me. I made them an offer. It was a small offer that involved absolutely no upfront money. I didn't have any money to give them. What I did have was the dream and I sold it to them. I offered them a small percentage of the company, in exchange for their members and listings. They accepted. We signed a letter of intent that same day.

The following day, Gold's sent an email to their members, alerting them that they would soon be transferred over to DutchBid. The response was tremendous. Thousands of members didn't wait to be transferred, they came and registered on their own. CNet got word and their headline read, "Small Net Auction Company Goes for Gold". This drew even more traffic to the site.

A week later, a slight hiccup. The owners of Gold's told me they were afraid to transfer the member base over to me for fear of violating their privacy policy and FTC regulations. My attorney assured them the way the deal was structured, it wasn't a transfer – I was buying the company and merely changing software. They didn't agree and, eventually, the deal went sour. CNet's next headline was "Gold's Merger a Tarnished Flop". Witty.

Despite the merger not coming to fruition, my site still received a lot of press and almost half of the Gold's users registered for accounts on their own. They also started listing items in droves. The Mitnick story was still being reported all over the Internet and was still bringing in tons of traffic.

I'd like to say this story ended with me making millions and eventually selling the company to some big corporation in Silicon Valley, but it didn't. My web hosting company was billing me quarterly. Things were much different back in the year 2000. Bandwidth was super expensive. DutchBid was also built on the ColdFusion platform, which was the most expensive kind of hosting, at the time. When February rolled around, I received a call from my hosting company's owner. He said he had never seen traffic like this and my server bill for January alone was $48,000. I nearly had a heart attack. I told him I didn't have that kind of money, but what I did have was a fast growing cash cow that was starting to generate money. He wasn't impressed. He wanted to be paid right away. I tried to make a deal with him, but it was cash or DutchBid goes away.

DutchBid went away.

In the end, I was no better at running an auction site than the folks at Gold's.

I often look back at those days and wish that I had known then what I know now. A site generating the traffic that DutchBid was in the year 2000 was surely worth a fortune. There are so many ways I could have monetized the traffic better, including simple banner ads that paid per view. Back then, targeted traffic was getting upwards of $9 per thousand banner views. I would have had tens of millions of views each week. There were also venture capital firms that were handing out money by the truckload. A few phone calls probably would have been all it would take to get some cash thrown my way, but I was still wet behind the ears and didn't know the slightest about the ways of the web, yet.

CHAPTER 6

ASK DANIEL NEGREANU

Fast forward a few months. With a little money in my pocket from the George lawsuit settlement, I was in no hurry to find another real job. Instead, I occasionally built websites for local businesses and played a lot of poker.

On the morning of September 11, 2001, I was sleeping on my couch. The phone woke me up. It was my mother asking if I had seen that a plane had hit one of the World Trade Center towers. I immediately turned on the television, just in time to see a second plane crash into the second tower. Like most of the world, I spent the next several hours glued to the TV. When I couldn't take anymore, I headed out to the casino. A bunch of us sat around the poker table talking about the events. All the TVs were on news channels. I felt the need to go back to my couch and watch more.

I have always been a news junky. Producing video in Somalia was the rush of a lifetime for me. I knew what had just happened in New York was going to change the world forever and I wanted to somehow be a part of it. News would be a good way.

The next morning, I called the news director at WLOX, the ABC affiliate in our area. We met that day and I started producing the 5:30 news a couple of weeks later.

A producer decides what stories will go into the newscast. In a small market, the producer also does all of the writing. I bang the words out on my keyboard and the anchors read it on TV.

I loved creating a newscast, but I kind of felt like behind the scenes wasn't the place for me. My anchor, Dave Elliot, encouraged me to make a demo of me reading the news behind the desk. I did and thought it went well, but it didn't matter. The news director wouldn't look at it. He said I was hired to be the producer. I was ok with that, as just loved being a part of the news team. However, it was taking its toll financially. The job paid dismally. My take home wasn't enough to pay my bills. I was using the George money to make up the difference The work days were long, so there wasn't enough time to do freelance stuff on the side. After just a few months, I had to quit and there went my career in news.

I went back to building websites and playing poker.

Back in 1991, when I found out Uncle Sam was stationing me at Keesler Air Force Base, I was a little uneasy. I grew up in Boston. We had everything from professional sports to enormous shopping malls and everything in between. There was always something to do. What would there be to do in Biloxi, Mississippi?

The answer was "not much". At least for a little while, anyway.

Shortly after I settled in, there was a statewide vote to allow gambling. Literally, one day after the measure passed and went into effect, the first casino opened its doors. Biloxi got interesting, fast.

I was the kid in fourth grade that got in trouble for making Super Bowl squares.

I was the kid in tenth grade that got in trouble for sneaking into the dog track.

I was a born gambler and Biloxi was now a gambling town.

Poker was always my big interest. You aren't playing against the house and skill always outweighs luck. It's the only casino game you can consistently beat, if you are the smartest player at the table. It's a game where your status means nothing. Doctors and lawyers can sit down and get outsmarted by high school dropouts.

Poker is also a subculture in its own. Poker players understand other poker players. It doesn't take years to bond with another poker player. Sharing a couple of bad beat stories can form an everlasting friendship.

I had decided my next online venture was going to be a combination of something I was passionate about and something that was profitable. Poker was both of those things.

My timing was perfect. It was about two years prior to the big televised poker boom, but there was an online poker revolution coming. I just felt it.

Despite the growing popularity of the game, there were very few websites dedicated to poker, at the time. My first step was to come up with a suitable domain name.

Every casino I played in often made announcements about their "live action poker games". I was pretty psyched to find that LiveActionPoker. com was available. I snagged it and began brainstorming about what to do with it.

Even though there weren't many dedicated poker websites, there were a couple of well-established authority sites that got a lot of visitors. I knew I had to do something to stand out and to show I was an authority in the industry.

Back then, the poker world was still small enough to where you could find a way to contact anybody, even the rising stars that were winning tournaments and writing books. That was my plan - to get together with the big dogs and gain authority by association.

This was the first time I used the "association" strategy, but certainly not the last. Throughout my career, I have gained authority in whatever niche I was working in, simply by associating myself with the rock stars of that field.

The first person I reached out to was a young Canadian who had won his first World Series of Poker bracelet a few years prior. His name was Daniel Negreanu.

Daniel agreed to do a podcast interview over the phone with me. After the interview, I talked about my plans for a chat forum and asked him if he would man a section of the forum called "Ask Daniel Negreanu". He loved the idea.

I set up a website that had a few articles and added a forum, using some free software. Word quickly spread throughout the poker community that you could chat with Daniel Negreanu at my site. And the people came.

Years later, when Daniel was an international television celebrity, I was speaking to him on the phone. He was with Toby Maguire at a tournament in Los Angeles. When I got off the phone, I told my young son the guy I was talking to was with Spiderman. He asked who the guy was. I told him it was Daniel Negreanu. His jaw dropped and said, "You know Daniel Negreanu?" Who would have thought there would come a time when little kids would be more excited about a poker player, than a super hero?

I followed the "Ask Daniel Negreanu" move by reaching out to more poker celebrities. Linda Johnson and Lou Krieger both manned sections on the forum and I conducted many interviews with poker royalty.

As traffic increased, I had to find a way to monetize the site. Online poker was still very new, but was gaining ground fast. I decided to sign up for a few affiliate programs and place their banners on my site. Every time somebody clicked on my banner and played for real money, I would get paid a commission of what the site made from that player or a flat fee.

As the months went by, the content on the site grew immensely. Thousands of visitors would read the articles and forum posts, each week. My income was also growing. I was bringing in a few thousand dollars a month in revenue from the banners. Life was good.

Then, it wasn't.

When I was in basic training, I couldn't understand why it was so important to make my bed so well or align my boots perfectly. Then, one of the drill instructors explained to me that it's all about attention to detail. He said, "Some of you will go on to be aircraft mechanics. The last thing you want to do is leave a wrench inside the engine of an F-16. Basic training is all about learning to pay attention to detail."

I guess it didn't take.

I woke up one morning to find Live Action Poker had been hacked. The homepage was a skull and crossbones with some Arabic writing. Tech support told me it was just a default index page that had been added to my site and all I had to do was delete that one page.

The control panel for the website was a bit confusing, but it did have a system in place where a pop-up window would appear asking if you are sure you want to do something, before it is finalized.

I stared at the window that said, "Are you sure you want to delete your entire site?" I read it twice. Then, I clicked on "Yes".

I don't think a millisecond went by before I said out loud, "What the fuck did I just do?"

Gone.

It was all gone. The articles, the tens of thousands of chat forum posts, the hours of writing effort put in by poker celebrities.

I called tech support.

"We're sorry, sir. You did not opt for the backup service, so we do not have any archives of your data."

I just put myself out of business.

After wallowing in my sorrow for about thirty minutes, I left the office and headed to the only place I knew that would make me feel better. I went to the casino to play poker.

I remember this poker game like it was yesterday. Three obnoxious tourists and four really old regulars. Whenever the games were dull or I had no desire to talk to the other players at the table, I would read a magazine and the only magazine to read in the poker room was CardPlayer Magazine. In fact, it was the only poker magazine in existence.

As I browsed through the pages, I recall thinking how poorly designed it was, how boring the articles were, and how I could do a much better job putting a magazine together.

Wait. Could I do a much better job? I didn't know, but I immediately cashed out my chips and ran to Office Depot.

"What's the best desktop publishing software you have?"

"We really don't have a big selection, but you can try Microsoft Publisher."

I bought it and rushed home to see what I could come up with.

And that's the day I became a magazine publisher.

CHAPTER 7

LIVE ACTION POKER MAGAZINE

Microsoft Publisher was pretty easy to learn. Pages were created using a "What You See Is What You Get" editor. In geek world, we refer to that as WYSIWYG.

I bought several magazines from the grocery store and began studying their layouts. Then, it was just a matter of copying the structure.

After the basic structure of the magazine was completed, I needed to fill it with content, so I reached out to some of the folks that were writing for CardPlayer Magazine. Most were very receptive to a new magazine being created and some even volunteered to write articles for free.

This was the year Chris Moneymaker won the World Series of Poker Main Event. This was significant, because Chris was just an average guy that won his seat to the big game by playing a $30 online tournament at PokerStars.com. Most of the other 800 entrants were professional poker players that paid $10,000 to play. When the world saw that a redneck from Tennessee could win millions of dollars without any startup money or professional training, the people rushed in. The fact that his name was "Moneymaker" helped too. Chris was booked on just about every late night talk show there was. All of a sudden, poker was mainstream and it was huge.

ESPN had been covering the WSOP for many years, but this was the first time people actually watched. The ratings they received were enough to convince the network execs to expand the coverage and shoot some of the smaller tournaments, as well as the main event.

Now, I needed to find a printer. I contacted a printing press in New Orleans that was willing to help me publish the magazine for a very reasonable rate. I couldn't afford to make all the pages glossy, so they suggested a gloss cover and newspaper pages for the guts. I wasn't crazy about this idea, but if that's all I could afford, then that's what it had to be. Now, I needed to get some advertisers.

The head of marketing for Poker Stars was a short bald guy named Dan. He was a nice guy, but had a touch of Napoleon Syndrome. Dan liked to be in charge and he liked to take credit for the explosion of the online poker industry, in particular, the site he worked for. The fact is that Dan was in the right place at the right time. Chris Moneymaker winning his seat to the World Series on his site was like a gift from the poker gods. Any monkey could have run the show and blew up the company with that kind of publicity.

I knew Poker Stars was now raking in the big bucks, so I reached out to them about buying some advertising slots. The key to selling a guy like Dan was to let him think all the ideas were his. I had every intention of putting Moneymaker on the first cover, but when Dan suggested that would be the only way he would buy my sponsorship package, I made it seem like I already had a different cover in mind for the premiere issue. We went back and forth, until I finally said, "OK, Dan, you win." We signed a three issue contract and my entire printing costs were covered by the first advertiser. The rest would be pure profit.

Once Poker Stars was on board, selling the rest of the poker sites was easy. They all wanted to follow the leader and I took full advantage of that. All the advertising slots were sold within a week.

I didn't forget about the website. I was still sick about losing all the content, but now I felt like I had a good opportunity to use the magazine to drive traffic to the new site. The new site would basically consist of an online version of the magazine and I would resurrect the chat forum.

Several pages were set aside to promote the website. I created a full page ad for the "Ask Daniel Negreanu" forum, letting everybody know they could chat with a celebrity.

The new site and magazine were ready just in time for the 2004 World Series of Poker. I had 10,000 copies of the magazine printed and was excited to get it out to the public. The magazines were shipped to Las Vegas and I was boarding a plane.

My finances weren't exactly as I had liked them to be, so this trip had a small budget. I booked a room for two weeks at the El Cortez Casino and Hotel. It was an old, rundown hotel in the downtown area, just a couple of blocks from Binions, where the WSOP was being played.

A few months earlier, I had met a man named Herb Van Dyke at a poker game in Biloxi. Herb was also an entrepreneur in the poker world. He was putting together a series of poker cruises and was in Vegas to drum up business. He and I hit it off and spent time talking shop.

Herb turned out to be very helpful, too. He assisted in securing a spot to give away my magazine that was right outside where the tournament was taking place. I had a ten foot table set aside just for my magazine. The night before the main event began, I neatly stacked out about a thousand copies.

The next day, Herb and I had breakfast at the Golden Nugget, before heading across the street to Binions. We were both excited to see two guys sitting at the corner booth, each reading a copy of the new Live Action Poker Magazine.

After breakfast, we headed over to Binions. It was packed full of poker players, fans, and even Hollywood celebrities.

The tournament area was non-smoking, so a few of us would sneak into the bathroom for a smoke. While taking one of those smoke breaks, I spoke to a guy with sunglasses and a baseball hat. His voice sounded familiar, but I didn't recognize it, at first. In mid-conversation I said, "Hey, you're Norm!" He acknowledged. Just then, my wife called my cell phone. I thought it would be funny if he answered for me. "Hello, this is Norm McDonald. I'm in a men's room with your husband. How can I help you?" My wife was not a Saturday Night Live fan. She had no clue he was one of the funniest newsmen in the history of the show, so she just thought it was weird.

When I approached my magazine table, I saw that all the magazines were gone. There were a lot of people there, but it seemed a bit fishy that all one thousand copies were grabbed up so early in the day.

It turned out they weren't. Just as I arrived at the table, so did a young Indian kid with a dolly full of magazines. He began stacking them on my table.

The magazine was called "All In" and was a large publication, with high quality gloss paper. It was in the style of *Cigar Aficionado Magazine*. In other words, this was a nice magazine.

I asked the kid what happened to the other magazines that were here. He said, "I threw those pieces of crap in the dumpster."

Herb saw that I was about to lose my shit and cause a scene, so he grabbed me by the arm and said we needed to handle this in a professional manner. I found the folks from Binions that offered the spot for me. They weren't very receptive. They said they had a tournament to run and I needed to deal with this myself. One of them snidely said to call the police. Well, this kid did take property of mine, so calling the police was actually not a bad idea.

An hour later, an officer arrived to take my statement. They flagged down the kid and he said he needed to find his boss. He returned with a young blonde guy named Kasey Thompson. Kasey asked me to step outside with him and talk about it in private.

He immediately apologized for what he called a "mishap". I corrected him and said it wasn't a mishap, it was destruction of property. The more irate I got, the nicer he got. This actually irritated me more.

Kasey explained to me that he had signed a contract that morning to be the official magazine of the WSOP. Later, it was confirmed this was the case. However, he offered to share the space with me, allowing me to set new copies alongside his. He also offered to make amends and take me out that night to a club with some poker celebrities. I later found out Kasey was a young millionaire who made his money by working with some dot com startup back in the late nineties.

That night, Kasey introduced me to Chris "Jesus" Ferguson, Phil Hellmuth and a few others that were the cream of the crop in the poker world. He even introduced me to movie star Ben Affleck, who I had just read was playing quite a bit of poker these days. Affleck was from Boston, too, and I knew he was a big Red Sox fan. I told him if I had a million dollars, I would bet him the Sox would win the World Series that year. He said, "If you had a million dollars, I would take that bet." Too bad for me, because they did win it.

Kasey knew everybody.

After many hours of $400 a bottle VIP service at various clubs, we ended the night at a small bar inside Bellagio Casino. There were about ten in our group, all incredibly wealthy, except me. Kasey started to make small bets with the other guys – and by small, I mean ten thousand dollars. He bet one dude he couldn't eat ten saltine crackers in under a minute. Apparently, that is something that just can't be done. Kasey took the large stack of hundreds he won and bet it all on one hand of blackjack. He lost and said, "Oh well."

This was my first taste of how the other half lived. How they were carefree with their money. How they did what they wanted, when they wanted. This was my glimpse of people with this kind of dough. Everybody knows that money can't buy happiness, but it certainly can get rid of some of those little worries most people have.

CHAPTER 8

IT'S NOT LACK OF FOCUS, IT'S EVOLUTION

Over the next two weeks, I spent a lot of time with Herb. We took notice of all the new poker related websites that were popping up, as the industry emerged. A lot of the owners were in Vegas, promoting their new ventures.

Some of the sites were focusing on video. They were conducting interviews with players and publishing them to their websites. This intrigued me, as video was my forte. After I watched some of the clips online, I told Herb I could do a much better job at this. I said I could probably put together a news style show that would blow away these awful snippets of bad interviews and shaky cameras. Herb told me to slow down.

"Are you a magazine publisher or a TV producer? You can't be both," Herb lectured.

Well, the truth is, I'm not really a magazine publisher. Ok, I was publishing a magazine, but come on. This was a thrown together thing I thought I could make a few bucks with. It was actually shocking to me that I was able to pull it off. I told Herb that I was having fun, but I knew I could really kick ass with video. Herb said I was lacking focus.

The next issue of the magazine was a breeze. I filled it with photos I had taken at the World Series and the articles were mainly recaps of the tournaments. My sponsorships grew, too. I had to add a few more pages just to fit the new advertisements, but all I was thinking about was video.

It was still a couple of years before the world would get swept up by YouTube. Video on the web was not an easy thing. It was also expensive. The bandwidth that video eats up can put a hole in your wallet. But I believed a poker news show could be very profitable.

I mentioned to Herb that it would be great to sell the magazine and use the money to buy the video gear I would need. Expecting him to tell me to quit dreaming, he actually responded positively this time. He said, "It's not a bad turnkey business to package up and flip. Give me a week. I'll find you a buyer." Ya, ok.

A week later, I called to razz him about not selling the magazine yet. He surprised me again by saying he thinks he may have. The next day, I flew to Virginia Beach to meet with him and his perspective buyer. Just ninety days after accidentally deleting my website and two issues of a thrown together magazine later, I left Virginia with a check for fifty thousand dollars. The new owners wanted to change the name of the magazine, so they allowed me to keep the website.

Not even 24 hours went by before I ordered my new camera and editing equipment. I registered the domain PokerUpdates.com and began putting together a simple site. While waiting for the gear to arrive, I created a press kit about the upcoming show. I highlighted my background in television production and the successes of my poker magazine and website. The kits were sent out to all of my previous sponsors.

Within a week, I had two sponsors on board, including the up and coming Full Tilt Poker site as the show's title sponsor.

One of the founders of Full Tilt was Howard Lederer. He and his sister, Annie Duke, were well known pros and Full Tilt was comprised of a stable of famous spokespeople. Howard called and asked me to come to Vegas to do a news story on his upcoming poker boot camp. This would be the first feature of the TV show.

While at Howard's camp, I mingled with several celebrities from the poker world and beyond. One of the first interviews I conducted was with Penn Jillette of the Penn & Teller magic duo and *Bullshit* TV show. Penn gave an entertaining commentary on Hollywood actors thinking they can play poker. He said, "They're actors. They don't write anything. They don't direct anything. All they do is what other people tell them to do. How the hell can they make a decision at the poker table?"

The next stop was Herb's poker cruise. I drove down to Orlando and boarded a Royal Caribbean ship, along with about a hundred other poker enthusiasts. Herb even hired Chris Moneymaker to come as the celebrity guest. More great footage and interviews.

That was two trips I was paid to take and the first episode of the show wasn't even out yet. I started feeling a little pressure. Could I really pull this off? If so, could I do it month after month? Eh, whatever. If it works, it works. If it doesn't, I'll move on to the next thing.

It worked.

Two weeks after the cruise, I had a finished thirty minute TV show for the Internet. I created a backdrop and used myself as the anchor. The news desk was an old table in the middle of my living room, but on video, it appeared I was in a million dollar studio. I had friends narrate the scripts for the news clips and the sponsors supplied their own commercials. The entire show was edited on my laptop, using Adobe Premiere software I had bought at Office Depot.

These days, an online show like this would be easy to get viewers for, but back then, we didn't have FaceBook and YouTube. "Going viral" took a huge number of people actually emailing their friends a link to your site. I had a lot of work ahead of me to get the word out about the new show.

Once again, I utilized Daniel Negreanu and his increasing fame. Daniel taped a segment called "Daniel's Corner", where he talked about the poker lifestyle. His first segment was about when he was starting out as a professional poker player. There would be days he won a bunch and his mother would be excited, but the days he lost a bunch, she would go apeshit. His solution was to tell her he won $200 five days a week and lost $200 the other two days. It didn't matter if he was up or down a grand, he always said $200.

Daniel had a blog site that was quickly gaining a lot of traction, so I asked him to blog about the new Poker Updates show. He did and a swarm of his fans came to watch.

As soon as the first episode was finished, I flew back to Vegas for another major poker tournament. I shot video and got interviews with the key players. The next episode of the show was uploaded exactly a month after the first.

People were watching. I checked the stats on the second episode and was blown away to see that over 300,000 people had viewed the show. When I returned to Vegas to cover the next tournament, people were recognizing me and saying how much they loved Poker Updates. It was quite surreal.

I began adding my own commercials. Some of the online poker affiliate programs paid pretty decent commissions and these commissions were recurring. As long as the players I sent kept playing, I kept getting paid. So, I created some incentivized bonus plans. If you registered and played at one site, I would send you a DVD of the movie *Rounders*. Register and play at another site and I would send you fifty dollars.

Because of all the travel involved, I was only able to produce one episode a month, but that was enough to make a solid living. Full Tilt Poker was paying me $12,500 per episode to be the title sponsor. Two other poker sites paid me $2,500 for thirty second commercial spots. By the fourth episode, the affiliate promotions I had running inside the shows were paying me around $5,000 a month and growing. My travel and video bandwidth expenses ate up about $10,000 a month. I wasn't rich by any means, but I was traveling, meeting famous people, and making enough to live on.

It seemed that all of a sudden, Poker Updates was a force in the growing poker media world. I started receiving invites to all the poker related parties and events, some of which had pretty well known people there.

The World Poker Tour called and asked me to cover their celebrity poker tournament in Los Angeles. It was filled with celebrities from the D List to the A. Linda Johnson, who I had become very friendly with after she wrote for my Live Action Poker website, was playing at the same table as Ray Romano. People have been telling me I look like him for years. When I approached her table to take some video shots, Linda told Romano that people call me "Ray" all the time. He stared me up and down and said, "If I was that ugly, I never would've ended up with my own TV show."

I met Lyle Berman while waiting for the valets to bring my rental car around. Lyle was the original investor of the World Poker Tour. He made his millions building casinos in Las Vegas and throughout the country, including one in my hometown of Biloxi. He said he had watched my show and wanted to meet with me if we were ever in Las Vegas at the same time. We exchanged numbers. That was kind of exciting, although I left him a few messages, but he did not return my calls. Months later, he called and asked me over to his condo for a meeting. It went well and he said he'd be happy "to throw a million at the project" if I was interested. Of course I was interested, but that ended up being the last time we spoke. He never followed up and my calls went unreturned. Maybe he got his jollies out of dangling carrots in front of entrepreneurs. Who knows. Nevertheless, it was exciting to know a big time industry maven was watching.

Everywhere I went, it seemed I was surrounded by TV and movie stars. It was hard to believe this was my life. It happened so fast.

One of my most memorable celebrity experiences was the birthday roast for Doyle Brunson, an old man that many consider the godfather of poker. It was a sit down dinner hosted by Brad Garret, who played the cop brother on Everybody Loves Raymond. Pamela Anderson was one of the roasters. Doyle was supposed to be the target of jokes, but Brad was fixated on Pamela. He started with digs about her stolen sex tapes and moved on to jokes about her having Hepatitis C. The digs got nastier and nastier and Pamela was visibly upset. When it was her time to speak, she crumbled up a piece of paper and threw it in Brad's face. She looked at the crowd, tears running down her face, and then stormed out of the room. Brad went back to the microphone and said, "Well that speech lasted longer than her career."

A week later, I cornered Paris Hilton to do a promo for my show. The next episode opened with her saying, "I'm Paris Hilton and you're watching Poker Updates." She ended it with her signature line, "That's hot!"

Things were moving fast. I was becoming well known in the industry and my income was slowly increasing. But I still look back and shake my head. Had I known then what I know now, I would have been making much, much more money. For instance, I had no idea the importance of creating an email list. I did not require any sort of signup to watch my show. You came to the website and the video played. In hindsight, I should have forced people to register. Then, I would have had a list that I could send direct offers to. That list would have been worth millions of dollars. Today, all the Internet marketing gurus say, "The money is in the list." Looking back, I could kick myself for not knowing this.

CHAPTER 9

THE MAN WITH THE PENCIL THIN MOUSTACHE

The traveling back and forth to Las Vegas and California for poker tournaments was taking its toll. My daughter was two years old and she needed Daddy around. My wife, Melissa, and I discussed moving to Las Vegas. We took a weekend trip to scope out rental properties, fell in love with a house we found, and moved within two weeks. My wife had always been open to my spontaneity and trusting that everything will work out. This is the kind of support every entrepreneur needs.

We still owned a house in Biloxi, but left it in the hands of a Realtor to sell. It was an average sized house on a cul de sac road. When my friends from Boston found out I had bought a house for $69,000, they thought I was living in a trailer. My friend, Hank, came down for a visit and couldn't believe what he saw. Back in Boston, that same place would be close to $400,000.

The house was on the market for a few months, before it sold. I made a very small profit by selling for $75,000. We did the closing via FedEx. Ten days later, Hurricane Katrina hit. Most people tell me how lucky I am to have sold the house just before the storm, but that wasn't the case. Other than a few shingles missing, the house made it through the storm remarkably well. That wasn't the case for most other houses. Remove half the homes from an area and supply and demand kicks in quickly. The new owners sold the house six months later for almost double their purchase price.

Katrina was devastating to the area. I couldn't help feeling bad that I was not there. I felt bad that I had friends dealing with the destruction and I felt bad that I missed the greatest weather event of my lifetime. It's the news guy in me. I had to see it, but I didn't want to be just a gawker. I figured out a way to help and sight see at the same time.

There were news reports that basic supplies were unavailable throughout the Biloxi area. I decided to go on a mission to deliver what I could. Since Biloxi was a poker town, I called on other poker players to help. I put a note on my websites asking for contributions. Within twelve hours, over $3,000 in donations had come into my PayPal account.

My old neighbor from the cul de sac was holed up in Memphis. I flew up there to meet J.J. and we began spending the money on everything from flashlights to baby diapers. Then, we made the drive down to the coast.

It was utter destruction.

The President Casino, where I hung my hat for many a poker game, was literally sitting on top of a Holiday Inn Express. The Grand Casino lay on its side, the highway littered with busted open slot machines.

The spots where century old antebellum mansions used to sit were empty, as if they had never been there - washed away completely by the 30 foot storm surge.

We videotaped the destruction and distribution of the food and supplies. Later, we created a short documentary and included it in the next episode of Poker Updates.

J.J. was divorced and just broke up with his girlfriend. I never liked her, anyway. She had originally left her husband and moved in with J.J., who lived right next door. This made neighborhood cookouts quite awkward.

When we finished in Biloxi, it was time to head back to Vegas. J.J. knew there was nothing left for him on the Coast and wanted to come with me. It was a good idea, as I needed another producer and J.J. had a background in television production. So, we drove cross country together. The house was quite large, so Melissa agreed to let him stay with us, until he found a place of his own.

By the time the 2005 World Series of Poker had rolled around, my online viewership was in the millions and people were taking notice.

The World Series was growing, too. There were tens of thousands of people there, mostly fans trying to get a glimpse of their favorite TV poker heroes.

I met Wayne Allyn Root at one of the various gala events. He was the host of a nationwide TV show where he and a team of retired NFL coaches would give their picks on the upcoming football games. He was known throughout the sports betting world as "The King of Las Vegas".

Wayne and I hit it off and spent a lot of time talking about the poker business and how it has exploded. He applauded my taking action and wanted to get involved more, himself. As I learned more about Wayne, I grew more and more intrigued. He was a self-promoter extraordinaire.

A month later, Wayne co-hosted one of the episodes of the show with me. Instead of my makeshift studio in my living room, we shot this one on location at a downtown Las Vegas casino. It was the best quality show thus far. He went on to create and host a show called King of Vegas on the Spike TV Network.

In the months leading up to our meeting, Wayne was getting active in politics, as well. He was lobbying for clarification on the laws of online poker, trying to get the green light that it was, in fact, legal. Wayne also became active with the Libertarian Party - so active they eventually asked him to be on the ticket as the Vice Presidential candidate. He ran in 2008 against Barack Obama and Joe Biden.

Wayne and I would often have lunch meetings to discuss our business ventures. One day, while eating at the Chinese restaurant in the New York New York Casino, we were talking about self-promotion and how important it is to your business life. Wayne mentioned how powerful branding was to his business. The term "King of Vegas" followed him around and helped him open the doors to many opportunities. I asked him who first called him that. Wayne's neck stretched out towards me. He looked around, as if checking to see if anyone was listening. "You don't know?" he asked. "I was." To this day, that conversation still rings in my ear. It was one of the most simple, yet important lessons in self branding I have ever gotten: Call yourself what you want people to call you.

Back at the World Series, all the characters were coming out of the woodwork. It seemed as if you couldn't go ten feet without hearing a pitch for some new poker related business that was going to take the world by storm. I interviewed one guy who believed a hat with infrared lights shining on your head was the key to being a better poker player. Another was trying to get investors for rolls of toilet paper with famous poker players' faces on it.

I was sitting at the bar, playing video poker when I first heard the voice. I say "the voice", because it is the most unmistakable raspy sound I've ever heard. Imagine a cross between Wolfman Jack and an old lady that smokes three packs a day. You know, the kind whose cigarette always has an inch of ash ready to fall on the carpet.

He was talking to another man about his new poker television network. He said his website was pokerTVnetwork.net. This caught my attention, because I had secured the domain name pokerTVnetwork. com just a few weeks prior. I didn't know what I was going to do with it, but just in case my little show blew up, I wanted to be ready.

He approached the bar to order a Coke. I told him I couldn't help but overhear his conversation and asked him about his network. He handed me his business card. It was cheap, made on a home printer. The card read "Steven Flower, CEO PokerTVnetwork.net". I asked him why he is using a dot net, instead of a dot com. Of course, I knew the answer, but wanted to hear it from him. He said, "I tried to register the dot com, but some asshole in Mississippi beat me to it." He reached out to shake my hand and introduce himself. "Steven Flower," he said. "Nice to meet you. I'm some asshole from Mississippi," I said back.

We spent the next few minutes talking about his vision for an online television network dedicated to poker. Unsurprisingly, all he had was a business card and a story. I walked away from the conversation thinking I would never see or hear from him again. I was wrong.

A couple of days later, Steven sent me an email telling me he had watched a few episodes of the show and wanted to talk about doing business together. My initial reaction was to roll my eyes and hit the delete button. An hour later, my phone rang. It was Steven telling me he had investors and was serious about joint venturing with me.

We met that night at his house. He lived in a neighborhood called Las Vegas Country Club. Back in the sixties and early seventies, this was the neighborhood to live in. His house was on the 15th fairway of the golf course. In fact, it was the same golf course where they landed an airplane in the movie Casino with Robert Dinero. His next door neighbor was Steven Adler, the former drummer for Guns n Roses. I had just watched a documentary on the band and it said Adler was a full blown crack addict. A few years later, I saw him on the TV show *Celebrity Rehab*.

The house appeared to be under construction. The kitchen was brand new, filled with expensive appliances and new granite counters. Two incredibly beautiful women were saying their goodbyes, as I was walking in. Steven was a short, skinny Italian guy with a pencil thin moustache. He was not the least bit attractive. I thought to myself, "He must be doing something right."

After the girls left, he brought me upstairs and showed me his office. His computer had multiple screens, all with some kind of stock trading program running on them. He said he was a day trader and had some

Wall Street friends that were looking to invest. My first thought was, "Here we go again." I didn't want another George situation.

Steven explained how he and a wealthy friend from Boca Raton wanted to buy my show and websites. They wanted to put some real money behind the business. He said they had plans to produce several more shows and build up a real network. They wanted my show and websites, because they already had a built-in audience. In exchange, they would give 33% of the company, a salary of $5,000 a month, and a third of the monthly profits. He said they would give the show a $200,000 budget to improve the production quality. Oh ya, he also had a check for $100,000, made out to me.

The most intriguing part wasn't the cash, it was that Poker TV Network took over a shell company, which was publicly trading as PTVN on the NASDAQ's over-the-counter-boards. A shell company is a corporation that is currently trading on the stock exchange, but really doesn't have a business set up. It is an easy way for a new company to slide in and begin trading quickly, without having to go through the red tape of an IPO. His offer included 33% ownership of the company. Although there was barely any trading activity, the stock was trading at over $3 a share. On paper, this deal was worth millions.

This was a tough offer to turn down, so I said yes.

CHAPTER 10

STRIPPERS, PROSTITUTES, & WEED, OH MY

I learned a few things about Steven real quick. The first was that he is loved his weed. I have nothing against people that smoke marijuana, but when I say he loved his weed, I mean the man smoked more than anybody I have ever seen. He would join the smokers outside. They smoked a cigarette, he smoked a joint. He smoked several times a day; in the car, outside the grocery store, at work, wherever.

Steven loved strippers. Prostitutes, too. He spent almost every night at The Crazy Horse, a small strip club that was near the Sahara Casino. He knew all of the dancers. Many of them were his friends. Whenever we would go to a poker event, he would have a beautiful girl in tow. He claimed he never paid them a dime, but I like to believe I knew better.

We found an office on Flamingo in the center of Las Vegas. It was three rooms, one of which would make for a perfect TV studio. I had a vision of bringing in famous poker players for interviews and how-to videos. I wanted to expand the brand and offer a series of tutorial videos that could be sold and downloaded.

A van full of Mexicans came to tear up the carpet and install a checkerboard floor. They came with a giant boombox and were remarkably fast. Studio lighting was installed in the ceiling. J.J. and I built a giant backdrop on wheels. On one side was the set design for my Poker Updates show, the other was a generic solid black. A control room was built behind one of the walls. This was the real thing. Life was good.

I wanted to get some media attention for the venture, so I had the idea to put together an advisory committee with a few key players in the poker industry. I set up a meeting with Nolan Dalla. He was a well-known poker author and the media director for the World Series of Poker. We were also friends. Steven insisted on going to the meeting. This was worrisome. Steven was loud. He was also stoned all the time. Often times, he didn't make a lick of sense.

The meeting started off great. I explained my vision for the show and the new network. Nolan agreed to join the board. Then, Steven had to jump into the conversation. He was touchy feely, slapping Nolan on the shoulder after each bad joke. It was embarrassing. Nolan later called and suggested I do something to calm him down or keep him away from people.

The next few meetings went similarly. I would make the good pitch and Steven would jump in and make us look like fools.

Another poker cruise was coming up and Herb had asked if we could do another segment for the show. Of course, I was happy to do it. There's nothing better than a free cruise. Steven insisted on going to that, too. It turned out to be more of the same. He acted a fool and I got taken aside by colleagues to tell me how bad he was for my image. To make matters worse, customs agents were called onto the ship and raided his cabin. They brought dogs to search for drugs and they found some. He smuggled a medicine bottle full of weed onto the ship. His cabin was in the same hallway the crew used to get to the bridge, so they were constantly smelling it burn. Instead of being arrested, Steven agreed to pay a civil penalty of $1,500 to the agents. He then made a point to tell as many people on the ship as he could about the ordeal, claiming his rights were infringed upon.

Things were getting bad. I had worked hard on getting into the inner circle of the poker industry and Steven was doing his best to undo it all.

Two months into our partnership, we still had not made another episode of the show. Steven's priorities were the parties and social events. While these events were important for making deals, any good we had to offer the industry was overshadowed by Steven's ridiculous behavior.

To top things off, J.J. was still living in my house, despite the agreement that he would come and start looking for a place to live right away.

I was having serious regrets about partnering with Steven.

Finally, I decided I was going to ignore him and all of his shenanigans. I was no longer going to take his orders and I was going to produce the next episode of the show. J.J. and I began covering events, conducting interviews, and editing video. We busted out a new episode of the show, fairly quickly. Steven didn't seem to care. He was upset that I was no longer telling him where the upcoming industry parties were.

It was time for Steven and me to have a talk. I went to his house and told him the sponsors were not happy. They were used to a new episode coming out monthly. The viewers were unhappy, too. The latest show only attracted about 20,000 people to the website. I told him things were going to have to change or we would lose everybody. Steven didn't care. He told me his investor asked him to shut the company down, so he could sell the "shell" to some computer business in Florida. My heart skipped a beat. I couldn't believe what I was hearing. I sold my business to these guys and they were just going to shut it down. Steven said he was working on changing the investor's mind, but I was not comforted. I immediately started thinking about how I could salvage what I had prior to the partnership.

I went back to work, covering poker events in Vegas and a couple in Los Angeles. J.J. got news that his mother had passed away and had to go back home for a week or two. I finished the next episode of the show myself. The viewers were starting to come back.

A couple of weeks later, J.J. returned. He was back from his mother's funeral, but he wasn't alone. He brought the ex-girlfriend and her teenage daughter along. I told him they could all stay for one night, but would have to find a place in the morning. One night turned into a week. The girlfriend acted like she owned the house, going as far as demanding we do her laundry. That was it. Melissa and I said enough was enough and we told them all to leave. We had enough problems with the Steven situation and didn't need this, too. We felt a bit taken advantage of.

Steven then told me the funding is running low and the company could no longer afford to pay J.J. He had just moved into his new place and, despite my frustrations with him, I did not want to see him without a job. I convinced Steven to let him stay on board a bit longer. Unfortunately, J.J. did not do his part to keep the job. He started coming into work hours late and sometimes not at all. When he did show up, he spent most of the time on the phone with the girlfriend. He no longer seemed interested in the job. At a celebrity tournament, J.J. messed up the audio during an interview I was conducting with my childhood hero, Roger Clemens. After that, I emailed Steven and told him the money could be better used elsewhere. I gave him my blessing to can J.J. My reaction may have been a bit fierce, but it wasn't just this screw up. It was a combination of everything. Plus, I knew this whole house of cards was about to come tumbling down. J.J. was going to be jobless, regardless of my email.

After he was fired, J.J. and I didn't talk for a while. He moved to Tennessee and the friendship had come to an end. It was a shame, because back in Biloxi, he was a good neighbor and a good friend. Years later, we were able to make amends and we have made a point to stay in touch.

I got a call from the folks at BoDog, an offshore poker and sportsbook website. They were shooting a TV show in Costa Rica that pitted amateurs and celebrities against professional poker players. They wanted me to come. At first, I thought they wanted me to come with a news crew to cover the event, but they wanted me to be one of the amateurs. They said I was well known enough in the poker world to make a splash as a popular amateur player. Unfortunately, my name came up late in the game and I was added as the alternate. If one of the confirmed players did not show up, I would be on the show.

Again, Steven insisted on going with me.

When we arrived in Costa Rica, Steven immediately disappeared. By the third day, I didn't know if he was alive or dead and I didn't care.

BoDog went all out, gathering a bunch of celebrities in one place. There weren't just poker celebs, there were Hollywood and sports stars, too. We all took a trip to the rain forest. I hiked through the woods with Jennifer Tilly, Willie Garson, Shannon Elizabeth, Chuck Liddell, and Cheryl Heinz. As a kid, I had always had a crush on Jennifer Tilly. At the time of the trip, she was around 50, but still looked like she was in her thirties. Cheryl is the one who played Larry David's wife on *Curb Your Enthusiasm*. She was very cool and we ended up hanging out a lot that week. Willie played the gay guy on *Sex in the City*. From what I could tell, it wasn't all an act. Shannon Elizabeth is best known as Nadia from the American Pie movies. She was just as hot in person as she was on the big screen. There was a guy wearing a Boston Red Sox hat. I asked him if he was a real fan or just one that jumped on the bandwagon after they won the pennant. He got upset and said, "Are you kidding me? Don't you know who I am?" I had no clue. He said, "I'm Boston Rob, what the fuck?" To this day, I still have no idea what a Boston Rob is. Apparently, he was on some reality TV shows.

Just prior to the show's taping, it was announced that BoDog owner Calvin Ayre would be on the cover of the upcoming annual Forbes Billionaires Edition. This was cause for celebration for their team, so a big party was scheduled for that night at Calvin's mansion. The problem was Forbes decided to go with the headline "Catch Me if You Can", referring to the gray line that online poker and sportsbooks operate under. We don't know if this was the reason, but Calvin's house was raided by Costa Rican police an hour before the party was to get started. They frisked and searched everybody there, including the Hollywood elite. When they found nothing, they left and the party went on. People speculated that somebody in Washington got their feathers ruffled by the daring headline and made a phone call. Sounds quite possible, but who knows.

There was one amateur player that had not yet shown up. He was being held up in Miami, due to an expired passport. He had just 24 hours to get things right and show up or I would be taking his place on the show. Needless to say, I was rooting against him, so I could get my shot.

Unfortunately, the guy was able to get his passport and showed up in the nick of time. I watched them tape the show from the sidelines.

Steven appeared on the last day, two Costa Rican honeys in tow. His eyes were crazy red and he smelled badly.

When we got back to Vegas, Steven dropped the bomb, making it clear that he and his investor friend were pulling the plug on the operation. They were selling the shell company to the computer business in Florida. The whole thing didn't make sense to me. Why would they invest money into buying my business, only to squash it and sell the shares in this publicly traded company? Later, my lawyer would tell me this was probably what is known as a "shell game", where they would fill a shell with a growing company, in hopes of it making headlines fast enough to dump their shares on the open market. Apparently, this can be very profitable, but rarely ever for the poor bastards that buy the stock. Or the company they targeted.

Steven declared that he was revoking my shares of stock, but was keeping his portion of the websites and whatever income came in from the affiliate programs. Say what? You bought my websites with millions of dollars worth of publicly traded stock, now you are saying you want to take back the stock, but still own the websites? I don't think so.

My salary was to cease immediately. I was not willing to walk away with nothing, so I said no to all of it. I was still entitled to 33% of the affiliate income and if a deal was to go down that involved selling of the stock, I should get compensated for the shares I owned. I explained to Steven that I rightly owned the stock and he could not just confiscate it from me. Steven disagreed. He said he gave it to me and he could take it away from me.

I still had thousands of dollars worth of personally owned video and computer equipment at the office. I grabbed a friend with a truck and headed down in the middle of the night to get my stuff. The locks had been changed. There was a note on the door telling me to give the stock certificate back now.

I got a phone call from Steven's investor, whom I had begun to refer to as "Mr. Investor". This was the first time I had spoken to him one on one. He was very loud, telling me bad things would happen if I didn't hand over the stock certificate. I didn't pay much attention to the threat.

I sensed things were going to get hairy and, once again, felt like I needed legal representation. I put a lawyer on retainer and told him to stand by.

I get another call from Mr. Investor. This time, his message was more clear, "You have two days to give the stock certificate back or you will be at the bottom of a hole in the middle of the desert." My lawyer asked if I thought he was serious. I did. He suggested I buy a gun. I did.

My hunch was that Steven was also getting pressure from Mr. Investor to get that stock certificate back from me. I decided to call Steven and tell him I would give the certificate back if he would give me access to the office and let me have my equipment. I was going to try and reason with him about how he is not entitled to anything if I give back the stock.

So much for that. When we met, he presented me with a document and told me to sign it or I get nothing, no equipment and no more compensation from the affiliate programs, which were now all in the company's name. The paper essentially made him my partner in the two sites that were driving in the bulk of the poker affiliate commissions. Mr. Investor no longer wanted a portion. I hastily signed. I needed my equipment, so I could move on with my life.

The following day, we met to hand over the stock certificate. I told him I was unhappy with the terms of the contract and felt I had signed it under duress. I also pointed out that his contract did not make any mention of the Poker Updates TV show or the domain names associated with the show. I presented him with a new contract. This contract clearly spelled out that he would give up any claims to the websites, the Poker Updates show, my equipment, and any future revenue. He signed it, without reading it, and I handed over the stock. He seemed relieved, almost like he would have done anything just to get his hands on that certificate.

When I got home, I changed the passwords on all the sites. I also changed the settings on the affiliate accounts, so all future payments would, once again, go directly to me. Steven no longer had access to anything.

It was just a matter of days before Hurricane Steven emerged. He tried to login and when he was denied access, he went on the war path. My phone rang, I let it go to voicemail. I can't remember exactly what he said in the message, but I'm sure you can imagine. The phone calls didn't stop. He left voicemail after voicemail, the tone of each getting more and more threatening.

I went to see my lawyer. We filed suit. This had to stop. Steven didn't like this. He filed a counter suit against me, claiming he was still entitled to half of all future revenues. He also began a barrage of postings to online chat forums and poker bulletin boards. He made claims that I was a thief and the poker sites I touted were rigged. He was doing his best to discredit and ruin the very sites he was suing to get his hands on. This is the mentality of an idiot.

I filed a motion for a temporary restraining order, asking the judge to bar him from continuing to make these posts. The hearing was very amusing. Steven was one of those know it all types of guys. He didn't like to take advice from anybody, so it was no surprise that he chose to represent himself. I have no issue with pro se litigants, but you really should know what you are doing, before heading into court. Steven didn't. He argued with the judge on every point. She scolded him several times, threatening to hold him in contempt if he didn't follow the rules of court. The restraining order was granted. Two days later, Steven began posting again. He didn't care that he could wind up in jail.

Steven filed motion after motion, causing me to have to appear several times in court. He lost each motion, but told my lawyer his goal wasn't to win, it was to force me to continue to keep paying high legal fees. It was working. I was deep in debt to the attorney and getting deeper.

A couple of months went by and I was still sitting in limbo. It was time I started to reclaim my life. I decided to move forward and tried to regain the status I once had in the poker industry. I busted out another episode of the show and managed to get a few online poker sites to come back on board as sponsors. Things were starting to look up. Despite the pending lawsuits, I was moving on and life was getting good again.

Then it wasn't.

In September of 2006, the U.S. Congress was in a heated debate over The Safe Port Act. The Act was designed to keep key U.S. ports from getting into the hands of foreign based security firms. There were over 20 revisions of the Act, until finally, one passed both the House and Senate. Unfortunately, there was an unrelated, last minute provision added. Title VII of the bill was called the Unlawful Internet Gambling Act of 2006. This essentially made it against the law to allow U.S. banks and credit cards to fund offshore gambling accounts.

The bill was signed into law by President Bush on October 13th. All of my sponsors cancelled their advertising deals, saying they had suspended all promotions in the U.S. Like that, my TV show was out of business.

The only silver lining was I still had a substantial amount of players outside the U.S. still playing on the sites I had affiliate programs with. This was now bringing in about $4,000 a month, which was certainly enough to live on while I figured out what my next venture would be. I was disappointed about the show, but I had money coming in and felt good about the future.

There was no longer a need for my family to be in Vegas, so we packed everything into a giant U-Haul truck and started to head home. On the second night of the trip home, we were settling in at a motel, somewhere in New Mexico, when I got a call from the company where most of my affiliate income was coming from. Due to the new laws and their loss of American players, they were closing up shop. This one company accounted for over 90% of my income.

With nothing left for him to come after, Steven stopped making motions. Eventually, both suits were dismissed for lack of activity. I just wanted to move on and it wasn't worth pursuing a stock certificate that I didn't feel would ever be worth a dime. My assumption was correct. Yahoo Finance is now showing that stock is valued at 0.002 cents a share. My share, which was once worth millions, would now be worth approximately $4,000.

A couple of years later and long after Steven was out of my thoughts, I got a call from a friend. He said, "You're not going to believe this." He then emailed me a link to a blog post made by Robin Leach from the show Lifestyles of the Rich and Famous. The post was about none other than Steven Flower. Steven was getting national media attention for an eBay auction for his house, his cars, his "model" roommate, and a rolodex filled with Las Vegas strippers. The story went viral in the media. Even the New York Post wrote about it in an article titled "Take My Life… Please". But even more interesting than the auction was another part of the story. Steven had been severely beaten by two men at a strip club in Las Vegas. He claimed to have been minding his own business when a group of men started an argument with him. I later learned that he filed a lawsuit against the men and the club for not providing adequate security. An online article stated he settled out of court with the club for one million dollars. However, the money doesn't make up for the fact that he now has a permanent limp and walks with a cane. Karma? Maybe. Funny? Definitely.

Steven's head pops up from time to time, just to harass me. The latest round came, coincidentally, as I was writing this chapter. A mystery man named Keith Overton, claiming to work for Steven, made several posts on FaceBook and my blog site. He told tall tales of how I owe him hundreds of thousands of dollars. Strangely enough, my investigator noticed that Keith Overton is the name of one of the men accused of beating Steven in that strip joint. "Keith's" last public post included my home address and the message my "day of reckoning is coming". He suggested I hide from what is coming. Idle threats of a deranged manic? Perhaps, but just to be on the safe side, I did file a police report. Apparently crazy doesn't cure itself, even after eight years.

CHAPTER 11

THEY MADE HUNDREDS OF MILLIONS

Back in Biloxi.

I spent the next few months making ends meet by building websites again. I felt like I had regressed back to what I was doing in the late nineties. My wife got her old job back teaching elementary school. A few months ago, I was partying with Ron Livingston from the movie *Office Space* and now I was meeting with real estate agents, begging them to let me build a website for them. I felt ordinary and I have always despised ordinary.

Poker was still huge on TV and an enormous amount of Americans were suffering from online poker withdrawal, now that many of their favorite sites stopped taking action from U.S. citizens. To me, this seemed like an opportunity, so I began thinking of ways I could legally tap into this hungry market.

Playing poker online for money was now considered against the law, but playing poker online was not. I thought, "What if I could figure out a way for people to play online for money and prizes, but without putting anything up for risk, thus taking away the 'gambling' aspect." Hmm. This could work.

I began by contacting several companies that had a hand in developing sites for casinos. To get a quality site that was comparable to the offshore casinos people were used to would cost upwards of six figures. I didn't have that kind of money, so I had to get creative. I thought if I could raise enough funds to properly promote a site, I could convince a software developer to partner with me. After a few weeks of pitching my case, it worked. I was able to find a developer in India that understood the potential and was willing to create the custom software necessary to pull it off.

My idea was quite simple. People could earn entries into online poker tournaments by completing offers. These offers could be anything from applying for a credit card to getting a free trial at Blockbuster. com or any number of other websites. Our company would be paid handsomely for sending would-be customers to these offers. In return, the customer would get free entry into the poker tournaments, which awarded cash and prizes to the winners. Legal online poker that paid, but without any risk to the player.

The next step was to raise enough funds to get the word out there. I needed money to market. The first person that came to mind was my old friend, Herb. As expected, Herb fell in love with the idea. He quickly threw out the name of a young poker player he knew that had recently cashed in some big tournaments on the poker circuit. He was what we called "cash flushed". The three of us had a conference call and then decided to meet up at Herb's place in Virginia. Herb and I made the good pitch and the young gun agreed to invest $50,000 into the venture.

I agreed to throw the pokerTVnetwork.com site into the mix. We would use it to drive traffic to the new poker free poker site. This put about six thousand dollars in my pocket and enough money to properly market the new venture. The development company was happy and began to build the software. We formed a new LLC, with each of us owning an equal share. The software company in India agreed to a non-ownership revenue share. I was tasked to oversee the software development, build the website, and quarterback the initial marketing. My two partners allowed me to take a modest $3,500 a month salary, until the site was generating solid cash flow. We were on our way!

Over the next few weeks, I worked closely with Raj, the owner of the development company. Raj spoke English, but his accent was very thick and I often had trouble understanding him, so we decided it was best to communicate through instant messaging.

Raj was no rookie at creating poker software. His team had many online casinos below their belt. Since the "poker engine" was already built, it was just a matter of customizing the software to integrate with the offers players would have to complete in order to gain access to the tournaments.

We decided on creating more streams of revenue by adding an advertising module. While players were competing in the tournaments, we would display banner advertisements on the sides of the game boards. An ad would also be seen while players were on breaks between tournament rounds. Our company would get additional revenue each time one of those banner ads were clicked on.

We called the site "PrizeDome.com". The software and website were ready for beta testing within a month. I reached out to my friends in the poker world and had them email all their contacts. On the first day, we had several hundred signups.

We began running nightly tournaments with small cash prizes to test the software. Within a week, these nightly tournaments were averaging about 200 players. Small bits of revenue from the banner ads was starting to roll in, too.

We started advertising and accepting signups for the first big "official" tournament. We were going to offer a $5,000 prize pool. To get into the tournament, you had to apply for a Visa credit card. Our company was going to make $120 for every signup that qualified for the credit card, which statistically is about 70% of those that apply. There was no doubt we could get a couple of thousand signups per tournament. I had dozens of credit card companies and other offers that paid similarly lined up for future tournaments. PrizeDome was going to be a money maker from the get go.

This was the first poker site of this kind that we knew of. There was buzz and people loved the software. Raj and I started talking about making a FaceBook app, so people could play inside their FaceBook accounts and the system would automatically invite their friends to play, too. This was going to be huge.

Herb and I got into a few scuffles about the software. He was a perfectionist and wanted it to rival the software of the big, multi-billion dollar poker sites. That was not going to happen with our small investment. The software tested well with our beta players. Once the company officially launched, there would be more funds available for constant improvement. Herb agreed. We also argued a bit about the structure of the tournaments and the prizes. It was small stuff that we eventually hashed out and moved on.

Then, out of the blue, Herb tells me our poker player friend and investor decided he wanted to pull out the remaining money that was in the company bank account. After servers, my small salary for running the site, and other costs, there was about $20,000 left. This was needed to keep the company rolling until the revenue started coming in.

Herb said he didn't understand it either. We can only assume that our investor had run into a few bad hands at the poker table and was in need of money. That's the problem with using gamblers as investors. They are all gung-ho when they are on a winning streak, but once the tides change, they want their money back.

Similar to my last situation, the investor told me he was still a part owner of the pokerTVnetwork website, despite dissolving the company. I said no way, Jose. The site was no longer generating any revenue, but it was pure principle. My giving up the site was part of a package deal that included investment in Prize Dome. You take that investment back, you lose ownership of my site. I was so tired of this kind of thing. Months later, I sold the domain on Flippa.com for $4,000. It was poison and I was happy to get rid of it.

This was becoming a trend. I would come up with a great idea, bring some people in, and watch it all fall apart. I was getting frustrated. And then there was Raj. This poor guy had a team of five programmers working on the venture for months.

I didn't have any enough personal money to invest in the operation and I was done with bringing investors into any more of my ventures. PrizeDome shut down and the world never got a chance to play free online poker for prizes. Oh, wait a second. That's not true. A few months later, a company called Zinga launched a very similar application and made hundreds of millions of dollars. Another missed opportunity. Another chance at becoming a millionaire slipped through my fingers.

CHAPTER 12

STARTING A $500K BUSINESS IN ONE DAY

My buddy, Bob Van Court, asked me to meet with a friend of his. He said this friend was interested in building a website for his company. I told Bob that I was doing my best to get out of the web building business and wanted to devote all of my focus on enterprise type web ventures that would continue to pay, month after month. He assured me that he had explained to them that I would likely only get involved if there was a partnership opportunity and this was correct.

After a little arm twisting, I agreed to the meeting. His friend owned a hearing aid manufacturing business. The business was in New Orleans, which was about an hour away from me. I figured I'd play a little poker at Harrah's while I was there, so that the trip wasn't a complete waste of time.

When I got to the city, one of the worst thunder storms in recent years started. My GPS couldn't catch a signal, so I called the office to get directions. The receptionist was about as dumb as a doorknob and directed me to one of the longest bridges in America. The problem was that the business wasn't on the other side of the bridge and I had to drive about ten miles before I could turn around, just to cross back.

When I finally arrived at the office, the parking lot was knee deep in water. I was soaked and pretty pissed off at Bob for talking me into this!

The guys told me they were interested in creating a new website, unrelated to their manufacturing business, and selling hearing aids online. I asked them about the legality of this and they pointed out a recent federal court decision that overruled the few states that had previously outlawed the sale of hearing aids online.

I had always thought that hearing loss varied from person to person, so I asked how they could sell a one-size-fits-all hearing aid on the open market. They explained that the most typical type of hearing loss is high frequency loss and that most patients suffering from this type of loss have a very similar audiogram reading. They would program their hearing aids to enhance that most common frequency loss. It wasn't a perfect science, but the majority of the high frequency loss customers would experience a major improvement.

I asked them if I could have a few minutes to do some research. After a bit of Googling, I found that there was very little competition, but a high demand for discount hearing aids online. Immediately, I thought back to all of the times where I had said, "I wish I knew in 1999 what I know now."

When we reconvened, I told them my interest in working with them on this, but made it clear that I would only get involved if I had a stake in the site. I gave them some details of my online marketing background and a taste of some of the things I could do for them. They responded by saying that they have changed their minds and then made it clear that they were only interested in paying a couple of hundred dollars to a web designer.

OK, goodbye and good luck.

The goal of every Internet marketer is to find a niche that is wide open, meaning there are a lot of would-be customers, but not much competition. I believed that I had stumbled upon such a niche and I wasn't going to let it get away.

During the drive home, I made use of my phone's voice recorder and recorded some notes on how an online hearing aid site could succeed. When I got home, I registered a relevant domain name that had the words "hearing aids" in it and started looking for manufacturers.

I found about a dozen manufacturers that were willing to take a typical audiogram of the average high frequency hearing loss patient and program the hearing aids as the orders came in. Three of them were willing to private label them for me at no additional cost. This meant I could come up with a new brand name and the devices I sold would have that brand name etched into them. Two of the manufacturers were willing to dropship, which meant all I had to do was take the orders and the manufacturer would ship directly to the customer.

I had several distribution agreements in writing within a couple of hours. My product costs were very low, especially compared to the extremely high prices that audiologists were charging their patients. The funny thing is that many of the devices were the exact same products the audiologists were selling.

My next step was to an purchase online shopping cart. A shopping cart is software that allows online customers to add products to a cue, while they continued to shop. When they are finished shopping, the click the checkout button and pay for their items. I was not a programmer, so I had to find something that was ready to use and didn't have a big learning curve. I bought the pro version of cart called CubeCart for $150.00 and began to fill it up with product pictures and descriptions that were provided to me by the hearing aid manufacturers. I set the prices of my instruments about $50 higher than what I was paying for them.

By the end of the day, I had a website, shopping cart, manufacturers, and my own private label brand of ready to wear hearing aids. I chose to call my new line of hearing aids "Rosebuds".

On day two, I did some keyword research and created an AdWords campaign. AdWords is the department of Google that is responsible for the advertisements you see when you "Google" something. You pick the keywords you want your advertisements to appear next to and then designate a price you are willing to pay per click. For example, whenever somebody would do a search for "hearing aids" they would see my ad, along with the ads of my competitors. The more money you bid for clicks, the higher up your ad appears on the Google results page.

Although there was little competition at the time, I was competing against some of the big companies and they were spending a lot. Needless to say, the cost per click wasn't cheap. This certainly made me nervous, but I was still willing to try. I set my daily spending limit at just $50. This meant my ads would continue to appear until I had spent $50. The ads would then be shut off and not appear until the next day.

An hour after my first campaign went live, I had my first sale. It was for two hearing aids. At the end of day one, I had made three sales and a $100 profit. I told my wife that if things go this well tomorrow, then I would scale up my AdWords campaigns and could be spending upwards of a thousand dollars a day by next week. She thought I was insane.

The next day resulted in the exact same... three units sold for a total of $100 profit. By the end of the week, I had scaled my daily ad buys up to about $200 a day. The profit margin was holding steady.

Throughout the course of the next few weeks, I tested different text ads and different target rankings. Targeting the ads that appeared on the side of the Google search results were costing me about $1.25 a click and targeting the ads that appear at the top of the search results cost between $3 and $4 a click. While those top ads were generating the most amounts of clicks, my cost per sale increased greatly.

Sales remained steady throughout the first six weeks, but I knew that there was a way to boost them up a bit, so I started thinking about my demographic. I was targeting older people that may not be as computer savvy as us youngsters. I wondered how many of them just flat out refused to put their credit card info online or were confused when the site took them to PayPal, so I made some changes.

The first change that I made was I got a merchant account and plugged it into my shopping cart. This made the payment process seamless. The user now never left my site when it came time to pay. This increased my sales by almost 5% in the first week.

The next thing that I did was get a $49 a month account with a company called OneBox. This provided me with a toll free number that I could forward to my office phone, cell phone, home, or wherever. I could set the times that I was available and send all calls outside that time direct to voicemail.

I placed the number on the top of every page on the site. I then got a virtual terminal from PayPal. This allowed me to take orders over the phone and type the customer's credit card information directly into PayPal, without having them make the purchase online.

Holy crap did that make a difference! My phone rang off the hook from that point on and my sales DOUBLED.

Doubling my sales was awesome, of course, but the downside was the fact that I was now tied down to being in the office or at least in a quiet place when the calls came in. No more going to the poker room during the day and laughing every time my Blackberry beeped.

I started to research how people were getting to my site. Was it all coming from AdWords or was I getting organic traffic too? Much to my surprise, I was getting a lot of traffic from regular searches. What were they searching for? They were searching for new brand name that I had created and was having private labeled. People were actually searching for "Rosebud Hearing Aids"!

This got me to thinking that a lot of people may have been turned off by the fact that my site was the only site in the world selling this brand of hearing aid. I put myself in their shoes and realized that I probably wouldn't buy a product of this importance that was only being sold at one place, so I figured that I had to change this.

The first thing I did was start creating more online shops. I registered dozens of hearing aid related domain names and started building them out one by one. I used different shopping cart solutions to keep them from all looking the same.

Pretty soon, there were dozens of "stores" selling my brand of hearing aid. I priced them all differently to keep it from looking suspicious. Essentially, I created fake competition and it worked. My sales increased dramatically. The bulk of sales were still coming from the main site that was advertising on AdWords, but the other sites would get sales, too.

Always thinking of ways to increase my bottom line, I started to add upsell products to my site's inventory list. I added batteries, cleaning devices, storage cases, replacement parts, and other related items. The replacement tubes and ear buds were huge sellers. The best part is that I got these items for free from my manufacturers, but sold them for five to ten bucks a pack.

I also created package deals, where you would get a free one year supply of batteries and replacement parts if you bought two hearing aids, instead of one. I created an exit splash screen. That's a screen that popped up whenever a visitor moused over the back button. It said "Wait! Get a free supply of batteries today. Call 1-800... and ask the operator how to get yours." I know that a lot of marketers don't like this sort of thing, but it got my phone ringing like crazy! I must of had at least two dozen people a day that started the conversation with, "How do I get free batteries?"

A few months down the road, one of my manufacturers told me that he was impressed with my progress and that I was now his biggest single buyer. I was outselling the audiologists and foreign distributors. BUT, he said that I was doing myself a disservice by charging so little. He urged me to test the elasticity of my pricing plan.

This seemed crazy at first. I was happy with the money that I was making and my initial thought was, "If ain't broke don't try to fix it", but I decided to give it a shot, anyway. I steadily increased my prices over the next few weeks and was shocked to see that my sales were actually increasing. By the end of about a month, I had doubled my prices on the hearing aids and just about doubled my sales.

The only thing that I can attribute to this price increase success is that so many people have the mindset that you get what you pay for and with my prices being low, a lot of people must have thought my product's quality was also low.

This business was started with a budget of less than $200 and was profitable in 24 hours. Less than a year later, I had thousands of customers and had generated almost a half million dollars in revenue. On the surface, this looks great, but in reality, things were going downhill.

Jaded by so many partnerships gone bad, I was insistent on doing everything myself. I was too gun shy to outsource my sales or even my customer support. My unwillingness to delegate any aspect of the business to anybody else was, eventually, the reason for the businesses decline. In the beginning, I was able to focus solely on sales, but as the customer base grew, so did the need for customer support. Spending all that time on the phone with current customers left little time for me to make sales to new customers.

And this wasn't your typical customer support. First of all, I was dealing with people that had a hard time hearing. Repeating yourself over and over again on every call took loads of patience. Then there was the age factor. To put it bluntly, older people can be quite grumpy. Some are downright mean. They also don't have a good understanding of how mail order returns work. Many would demand a refund before sending the product back and if they didn't get it, they would call their credit card company and file a chargeback. I would almost always win those chargeback cases, but each chargeback costs a minimum of twenty dollars and a high percentage of chargebacks (anything over 1%) can cause you to lose your merchant account – and get put on a blacklist, which prevents you from getting another merchant account for years to come.

Most of my customers were great. I enjoyed getting emails and letters in the mail telling me how my products have changed their lives for the better, but the stress of those that weren't satisfied outweighed that joy. Old people like to write letters when they are unsatisfied. I once got a knock on the door by an investigator from the state district attorney's office. They received three or four complaints and sent somebody to see what was up. The investigator checked my records and agreed that I was correct in how I dealt with all of the complaints, but the incident left a bad taste in my mouth. What would my neighbors think if they saw investigators knocking on my door? What would my family think? I felt like a criminal, when all I was doing was trying to make a living selling a product that actually helped people. I was starting to think I was not the right kind of guy to run a company that dealt with old people.

I was proud of myself for creating this business from scratch, but it was time to take a hard look at how it fit with my life. This was the least glamorous business I had been involved in. It did nothing to feed my need for a spotlight and it was becoming very stressful. The business was sound and with a little tender loving care, could easily be turned into a multi-million dollar company. But I wasn't the guy for that job, so I made the decision to sell.

I had decided that I was just going to sell the websites, but remain the distributor of my private label hearing aids. This would free me from having to deal with truckloads of customers, but still put some money in my pocket being the distributor to one person.

I listed the main website on Flippa.com, an online auction site that specialized in sales of websites and online businesses. I started the bidding at $1 with a reserve of $100,000. This meant that I was not required to sell, unless the bidding reached that reserve price. I knew the business was worth much more, but I wanted out and out fast. Within a few days the bidding was over $20,000. I thought for sure that I would reach my mark by the end of the auction, but it peaked at $39,000. I thought about relisting the site, but before I got the chance, I received a call from a guy named Jon Stoddard. Jon was very enthusiastic and felt he could knock it out of the park, but he wanted the Rosebud label, as well. After a couple of weeks of his due diligence, I agreed to his terms and sold the business to him for $100,000.

For some reason, I seem to attract a never ending parade of douchebags. Jon paid $60,000 up front and was making monthly payments for the remaining $40,000. After about six months, the payments stopped. I received a letter from his attorney stating that he felt he was deceived by the potential of the site. This was absurd, as there was never any promise of how much he would make. The lawyer demanded that I release Jon of any future payments and call it even. I said, "Hell no," and filed a lawsuit in Jon's home state of Arizona.

Arizona requires mandatory arbitration for any cases below $50,000. This meant the case would be heard by a magistrate and I would be allowed to participate in the hearing via telephone. My friend, Rich Wilens, had recently moved to my hometown and he had a long history as a legal professional. Together, we decided that I could win this case by representing myself.

During the hearing, I stated my case. I told the magistrate about how I stayed on board for thirty days to help with a smooth transaction. During those thirty days, Jon often called on me to help him make a sale. He would patch me through on a three-way call with the would-be customer and I would close the deal for him. When I questioned Jon, during the hearing, I brought this up. I asked, "Would you agree that I was a better closer than you?" He said, "Yes." I asked if that could be the reason why I made more money at this business than he did. Again, he said, "Yes." This seemed like it was the tipping point in the hearing. The magistrate sided with me and Jon was ordered to pay the remaining amount owed, plus court costs. His lawyer seemed very embarrassed. After all, he lost to a guy that didn't even have an associates degree, let alone a law degree.

As tolling as the hearing aid business was on me, it was also very rewarding. I made some good money running the company and put some cash in my pocket with the sale. The lessons learned were also invaluable. I had put together a game plan that could be duplicated in many different markets. I could easily start a similar business and private label any number of products. This game plan could work for exercise equipment, food products, beauty products, and electronics. If nothing else, the knowledge I picked up was a good insurance policy that would guarantee I would never be unemployed.

As for the private label line of hearing aids I created, Rosebuds are available for sale at many online retailers, including Sears.com. I guess Jon eventually figured out how to close deals.

CHAPTER 13

GOOGLE'S MAGIC WAND

A while back, while Googling this or that, I noticed some websites would come up in the search results with a picture. It turned out these were called "blended results" and those website listings were being pulled from recent submissions to Google News.

Google News is nothing more than an aggregator - meaning it pulls news stories from various websites and compiles a list of links to articles that are relevant to what the user is searching for – but it is super powerful for getting traffic and traffic to your websites is the key to monetizing. If you were searching for a given topic, wouldn't the listing with a picture grab your attention faster than the listings without pictures?

At first I thought the news section was reserved for big guns like CNN and MSNBC, but then I started to notice that there were a lot of news sites that I have never heard of. These were small, independent sites, some that were isolated to news about one particular niche. I found news sites that were specific to finance news, sports news, and just about any niche news you could think of. I even found approved news sites that were all about the porn industry. These sites appeared like they could be major news organizations, but my gut feeling was they were small sites, run by guys like me and I wanted in. I wanted my listings to show up fast and with a picture.

There was very little information out there about becoming an official "Google News Site", so I winged it. I made my poker site look "newsy" and I applied via Google's online application form. Several days later, I received an email from the Google News team telling me my site was not approved and would not be indexed in the Google News directory. Bummer. I moved on.

Now that I had some money in the bank and time to work on new projects, I decided to take my goal of becoming a Google News publisher off the back burner and really see what it would take to get a site listed.

It made my mouth water thinking about the amount of traffic you could get from having an approved Google News site. Ordinarily, when you post something to the web, you have to wait for the page to be indexed and then you have to hope that it gets ranked high, so people will actually find your site. Sure, you can help the process by creating backlinks from other pages or getting other website owners to post links, but all this takes time. When you are a Google News approved site, you post and it gets ranked within minutes! Sometimes you only get ranked for a few days, but you can rank with keywords that you normally would not have a shot at getting ranked with, due to the huge number of competition. You could easily get tens of thousands of clicks to your site, even if you are only appearing on the front page for a few days. In short, being Google News approved is a goldmine.

I started by digging up that old email from the Google News team. It had some notes about why I was turned down. The biggest objection was that my site did not have a corporate tree. They assumed all articles were written by one person and Google News approved sites had to have multiple authors. They also said that much of my content was not "newsy". They were right. Many of the articles were about how to play better poker or where to play. News articles are usually dated. They tell the who, what, when, where, and why about something that happened recently. Evergreen "how-to" articles do not qualify as news.

The first move I made was to start over with a brand new site. As nice as it would be to get a ton of traffic to a poker specific news site, I started thinking about how much nicer it would be to be able to send loads of traffic to any niche I wanted, so I decided to make a general news site and take a stab at getting it approved as a Google News site. It would be similar to a newspaper or one of the big dogs, like CNN. I would have different categories of news, so I could figure out which categories made the most money and focus more on that category.

The plan was to monetize the site with Google's AdSense program. When I sold hearing aids, I would buy ads on Google's AdWords. AdSense was the opposite of AdWords. With AdWords, companies paid to have their ads appear on search results and on websites that were associated with that company's niche. The company pays Google every time somebody clicked on one of those ads. AdSense allowed website publishers to add those advertisements to their websites. Every time a visitor clicks on the ad, the company placing the ad pays Google. Google, in turn, pays the website owner where the click originated.

AdSense ads in certain niches pay publishers a lot more than others. For example, if you had AdWords on a site about dogs, the ads that appeared would not pay much when they are clicked on. However, if you had a website about home loans, the advertisers in that niche pay a lot more per click, so you, as the publisher, would get paid more from Google when those ads were clicked on. The best part is you don't have to change the ads manually. You simply add some code to your website and Google automatically displays ads that are relevant to the content of each page on your website.

Many of the Google News approved sites that I looked at were publishing on software called WordPress. WordPress is free software that allows you to customize the look and feel of your site and the way you deliver your site's content on the web. It is easy to use, so many folks use it for their personal and business blogs. With the right "theme" installed, you can make your website look just like a news site. I found a company that offered WordPress themes specifically for news sites. I bought one of those themes for around fifty dollars and began to populate it with news articles in the various categories I added. To comply with the requirement for multiple authors, I sought out some folks willing to submit articles, in exchange for links to their respective websites, similar to recruiting guest bloggers. I also came up with a few different pen names for my own articles and created an online profile for each. Once I had quite a few articles published, I applied again. A few days later, I received another denial letter.

I made changes and applied again and again. Each denial letter contained details about what I had done wrong. Tweak and reapply. After many denials and many tweaks, I had just about given up. I decided to take one last stab at it before moving on. The next email I got from Google might as well have been a blank check. Approved! The letter said Google News would start indexing my news articles within 48 hours.

A couple of days later, my first article appeared in Google News. I remember literally jumping up and down from excitement. I spent the next week testing the best ways to make my articles appear in Google's regular search results. It wasn't hard at all. The trick was to include the keywords I wanted to rank for in the titles and content of my articles. This wasn't rocket science. It was the same as any other website publisher trying to rank in the search engines, only I had a secret weapon that made my sites appear within minutes on page one of Google's search results... and with a picture! It was exactly as I had imagined it would be. It was like I had a magic wand that brought tons of traffic to whatever article I wanted!

Over the next few weeks, I worked on monetizing the traffic I was receiving. One of the best methods I discovered was what I would eventually call "The Oprah Effect". I would watch The Oprah Winfrey Show and write short articles about whatever topic she was discussing. If she did a segment on some rare medical condition, I would quickly Google some info about that ailment and throw together a news blurb about it. As long as I kept it "newsy", it was OK for Google News. By the end of Oprah's segment, I would have my article published and swarms of traffic were coming to my site. The ads being served up by AdSense on medical related articles paid pretty well when they were clicked on. Oprah had some sort of magical spell on people. Whatever she talked about, people wanted to know more about. That is why I called this method "The Oprah Effect".

Oprah's book reviews were a goldmine. As she was giving her thoughts on a book, I would grab a few quotes from her and quickly write up a news story about Oprah's review. I would also include a link to Amazon. com, where you could buy the book directly. This link would be my affiliate link, of course, and that meant I would get paid a commission each time somebody clicked and made a purchase.

This was all happening around the time of the real estate meltdown. Banks stopped lending money and millions of people were in danger of losing their homes to foreclosure. The real estate crisis was a hot news topic and one that produced a lot of high paying AdSense ads from banks and lenders.

This was the most fun I'd had while making money. I was literally getting paid to watch TV and write about what I saw! After a couple of months, I was averaging revenue of a couple of hundred dollars a day. I worked when I wanted and I relaxed when I wanted. This was like a dream come true. Google News was a magic wand – I write, publish and article, and the people would come. Magic.

CHAPTER 14

TEACHER

While sitting at a bar, watching a football game, a friend was quizzing me about what I do. I briefly explained the Google News concept and how I struggled to get accepted. He asked if I could show him how I eventually got approved, so he could have a Google News approved site, too. He seemed genuinely interested, so I told him I would write out a checklist for him.

Three weeks later, I got a call from that friend. He told me his site was approved and he was now a Google News publisher. I couldn't believe it. This guy had never created a website before. He wasn't even a writer! All I did was jot down some quick tips on writing news articles and the steps he had to take to make a website that was acceptable to the folks at Google. That was all it took to turn a guy with zero online experience into a guy that was making easy money on the Internet. Little did I know, but this checklist I wrote would be the gateway to a new world for me.

I thought about all those hours I wasted looking for information about becoming a news publisher, but found nothing. If there was a book, an eBook, or anything I could have bought that would have showed me the way, I would have gladly pulled out my credit card. I asked my friend if he would have been paid money for the checklist I created. He said, "Absolutely!"

The checklist I gave my friend was pretty basic. It was a ten step process I jotted down into an email. I decided it would be really cool if I could turn that process into an eBook and sell it to the masses. Surely, there were other people searching for this information.

I started by copying the ten steps into a Microsoft Word document. Then, I expanded each step into a few paragraphs. I added screenshots and other images that gave a visual reference to what I was teaching. The eBook was complete, but it had a very clinical feel to it. I decided to humanize it a bit by adding an introduction that explained my own frustrations I had trying to get this information. From start to finish, I invested about two hours into the creation of this ten-step, 25-page eBook. I clicked the save button and I was finished.

I had never sold an eBook before, so my first challenge was finding the proper venue. Should I create a website and hope for the best? Sell it on eBay? I really didn't know the best answer, so I Googled it. I remember specifically typing into Google, "Where to sell an eBook". The first result I got was a link to a post on a website called "Warrior Forum", a chat forum for people doing business online. The post was from somebody like me who was asking about where to sell his newly created eBook. The first reply said something like, "If it is geared towards other Internet marketers, you should sell it as a WSO." Other people echoed those sentiments in later replies. What in the world was a "WSO"? It turned out a WSO was a listing in the Warrior Forum's "Warrior Special Offer" section. This was pretty much an online classified ad section of their website where people could list their eBooks, software, and services.

The WSO section was filled with pages and pages of products for sale. Many of the titles were very cheesy and screamed the all too familiar "get rich quick" type slogans. My first instinct was to run for the hills, but I decided to stick around and investigate further. It turned out that within the sea of crazy titles were some very useful products, many of them in the form of eBooks. Most of the products were priced low, around the $7 mark. Some included videos and were priced slightly higher. There was software too. That first day on the site, I bought several products. I bought an eBook that showed a few different ways of finding lucrative topics for AdSense monetized sites. I also bought software that worked with WordPress and made my AdSense ads look better on my news site.

Visitors were able to correspond with the sellers by posting questions and comments, below each ad. The site showed the number of times an ad was viewed and the number of replies under each one. It was a lot. There was a ton of traffic coming through this classified site. Some people had multiple products for sale and raving fans posting positive reviews beneath each listing. I used the search feature to look for products relating to Google News. There were many products that taught you how to drive more traffic to your sites and even how to monetize that traffic, but not a single entry relating to Google News. It seems as though I had a fresh topic to introduce to this group.

I didn't want to just show up and start selling something. I figured it would be better if I became a member of the community first. I did that by participating in conversations in the main part of the forum.

When someone would ask a question, I would try and give a helpful response. Often times, I had no idea what the person was talking about, so I Googled it, found the answer, and posted my response. This killed two birds with one stone: I was looking like a hero by providing answers to people's questions and I was learning myself. Why these people just didn't Google their own questions first is beyond me.

There were a handful of people that stood out as rock stars. They were very helpful and provided insight about their marketing experiences and answered a lot of questions from newbies and intermediates. Much of the information was regurgitated from one "expert" to the next, but the newbies couldn't tell the difference and they were appreciative of the answers they received. At first, I thought these rock stars were just knowledgeable people that had nothing better to do with their time. I was wrong. They had the same mindset I did. Their motivation was to get a good enough reputation so people would want to hear more and buy their products they had listed as WSOs.

My eBook was ready. The only thing left to do was come up with a title. A few weeks earlier, I had met a guy on the Warrior Forum, named David Eisner. He and I exchanged a few messages and our phone numbers. The first conversation we had was quite comical, now that I look back at it. He was telling me about some of the projects he was working on and using marketing jargon that I had never heard. As he was talking, I was Googling, just so I could keep up with the conversation. I told him about my project and he asked me what I was going to call it. I didn't have a clue. We brainstormed and came up with a list of potential names. In the end, I chose a name David had come up with: Google Red Carpet. I added the subtitle of "Your VIP Pass to Google's Front Page".

Back in my radio days, we all used stage names. I went by the name of Rich Dennis. Names with three syllables always rolled off the tongue better and were more memorable to the audience. I wanted the same for my eBook. I decided to use a shorter version of my real name, Eric Brian Rosenberg. Growing up, friends called me "E", "EBR", and "Rose". E. Brian Rose was the pen name I chose for the cover of that first eBook and it is the name I have gone by ever since.

When I felt I had enough clout in the forum to market my product, I started working on the advertisement I would place in the WSO section. Back then, most of the listings there were very basic. They were text only ads that gave a description of the product being sold. Boring. The forum allowed the use of pictures and even videos, but very few were taking advantage of this. I wanted my listing to stand out. I wanted there to be a wow factor.

The first step to the wow factor was proving the contents of my eBook worked. The best way I could think of to demonstrate this was to make a video in real time of me posting an article to my website and it appearing on the front page of Google within minutes and with a picture. I used free screen capture software, called CamStudio. It captured everything I was doing on my laptop and turned it into a video that I could upload to YouTube and embed into my ad listing.

The next step was write the sales copy. Many folks think an advertisement is just a bunch of words thrown together to describe a product. That's one way, I guess, but real copywriting is an art form. I'm no artist in that sense, but I at least knew that I should make my copy into a story that the readers could relate to. I told the story of how stumbled upon these blended search results and how I wondered how I could be one of those sites, much like I've described in this book. I added pictures and embedded my videos. To dress it up even more, I found a guy online that created graphics. He charged me $60 to make an awesome header for the ad that had a red carpet and a cool looking VIP pass. In the end, my listing told about a problem (need more web traffic and income), gave a solution (Google News), and explained how my eBook was the road map to getting a Google News approved site. I also included some testimony of the income I was personally generating by using the tactics outlined in my eBook.

I then signed up for a website called Warrior Plus. This was an online service specifically for folks selling products on the Warrior Forum. For $19, Warrior Plus would track the statistics of your sales, but more importantly, Warrior Plus integrated with autoresponders to collect email addresses from everybody that paid you via PayPal. An autoresponder is a service where you can add a substantial number of people to an email list and send messages to them all at the same time. You can even set it up to automatically deliver a series of emails at different intervals, based on the day and time a person is added to the list. Collecting the email addresses of your buyers is essential, so you can market more of your products or even share reviews of products that you get a commission to sell. At the time, the autoresponder service I used was called AWeber.

Everything was set and I had an eBook I believed people would want to read. I added my listing to the Warrior Forum and paid the $20 listing fee. Then, I waited.

Less than one hour after posting my first eBook, I had 11 sales. I also had my first review:

> "*First and foremost if you are looking for a fluff filled guide, go someplace else. The [author] has provided a FULL, DETAILED step by step solution to creating these sites. From creation to installing your theme and getting content and even how to get accepted by Google News.*"

Minutes later, another review was posted:

> "*This is one of the most precise set of instructions to build and promote a site I've ever seen. The author truly leaves nothing out.*"

The days and weeks that followed drew more of the same: sales and positive reviews. The product even attracted the attention of Mike Lantz, who is the owner of Warrior Plus. Mike made my eBook "WSO of the Day" and he mailed the link out to all of his members. This resulted in a couple of hundred additional sales.

Needless to say, I was quite pleased with the results of my first eBook. I had sold several hundred copies and had an email list of buyers. In the meantime, I still had my Google news site and was aggressively testing new ways to monetize it.

After several weeks of testing out new monetization methods. I decided to write a follow-up to my eBook. This was a short report that gave the results of my testing. I emailed my list of buyers and gave them a PayPal link to purchase the report. This resulted in a few more thousand dollars worth of sales. I was really loving how easy it was to create a product and earn money from it. I was also loving the fact that I was helping others.

Out of the blue, I got a phone call from a guy named Justin Quick. He said he was the assistant to James Jones and was interested in talking to me about doing a webinar with them. A Webinar? Hmm, I had heard of those, but couldn't honestly say that I had actually watched one. I told Justin I was interested in talking more, but would have to call him back. This bought me some time to Google webinars and James Jones.

It turned out that James Jones was leading the way with webinars in the "Internet marketing" niche. He had a huge following and was well respected. Apparently, landing a webinar with James Jones in 2010 meant you could expect several thousand dollars in your pocket.

A webinar is a seminar conducted online. There is a presenter and an audience, just like a real seminar, but the audience is at home, watching on their computer. Before I called Justin back, I spent a few hours watching replays of some old James Jones webinars.

The next time we talked, Justin brought James into the conversation. The two of them told me they wanted me to build up my Google News eBook and turn it into a membership site with videos and tutorials. They said they thought the product could sell for upwards of $500 plus $19 a month via webinars. While I liked the idea of the membership site, I thought the idea of people paying $500 for my information was absurd. I almost said no to them. I didn't want to embarrass myself by making an offer that nobody bought, but Justin was persistent. He said the IM world had never seen anything like this and he was confident that it would sell. OK, it was worth a shot.

I spent the next couple of weeks building a WordPress based website. I started by adding the content of the original eBook and the follow up report, then created videos. The videos were basically the same information, only me reading the content out loud. I used simple video editing software to overlay screenshots and images to support what I was saying. To make the site interactive, I added a chat forum, so members of the site could share their own experiences and ask questions. The chat forum was easily created by adding a free WordPress plugin, called Simple Press.

Once the website was complete, I had to get started on the webinar presentation. Most webinars were using PowerPoint slides to create their presentations. This was sufficient, but I wanted to make my presentation stand out a bit. Many of the webinars I had been watching were dull – white backgrounds with loads of text on them. I found myself reading ahead on the page and not paying attention to what the speaker was saying. I decided I was going to use less text per page, only sharing exactly what I was talking about. I had a hunch this would keep the viewer more engaged, instead of them seeing what I was going to talk about, before I started talking about it. I also added many pictures, some of which were off the wall, funny, or even a bit scary. This is what you call a "pattern interruption". It's not what the viewer expects to see and this results in more engagement.

The way webinars usually work, the host introduces a guest to make the presentation. For example, Joe approaches a well named marketer named Suzy. Joe says he has an awesome presentation and product to offer that he believes would be compatible with Suzy's audience. Joe and Suzy make a deal to split any revenue generated by the webinar. Suzy would then use email, blogs, and social media to invite her followers to the presentation. Here's where most marketers make a mistake: When the webinar begins, Suzy introduces Joe and Joe takes over, giving his presentation and sales pitch. Suzy doesn't make another appearance until the very end, just to thank Joe for the presentation. This is wrong, wrong, wrong.

Maybe it's the radio guy in me, but I believe the host needs to remain engaged in the conversation, throughout the entire presentation. All of the viewers of this webinar are there because Suzy invited them. They trust Suzy enough to be on her mailing lists, be customers of her products, and read her blog posts. This is why it is very important for Suzy to remain engaged in the presentation from start to finish. Suzy's audience doesn't know Joe. They have not built a trusting relationship with Joe. He is a stranger to them.

When James and I discussed my upcoming webinar with his followers, I made note of these concerns. I told him he needed to be included in the discussion throughout my presentation. I told him it's one thing if I, a stranger to his audience, said this is the best thing since sliced bread, but a much more powerful thing if James reinforces that statement with, "Wow man, you're right, this IS the best thing since sliced bread." James agreed. He and Justin would be on the webinar with me and would be giving these types of positive reinforcement statements throughout the presentation.

I began practicing my presentation. I recorded and played it back several times, making notes on where I dragged on or where a PowerPoint slide didn't make sense. I made a list of possible questions the audience may have and came up with answers. I wanted to be prepared. James offered his own suggestions and helped me tweak a thing or two. After a couple of days, I felt I had a solid webinar that was entertaining and informative. I was a little intimidated about the closing portion, though. The close is where you introduce your product and tell the audience to buy now. James suggested a drawdown style of close. This is where you give a high price and then a reason why you decided to slash that price down. We did this several times, eventually revealing the actual offer price. We decided on a price tag of $199 for the first presentation. Buyers would pay the $199 up front for instant access and then a recurring fee of $19 a month for continued access to the site.

James mailed the invites to his email list. It was a couple of days away. I bugged him repeatedly about how many people have signed up for the webinar. I was excited. When we started, there were about 800 people in attendance. Wow. I should have been nervous, but I wasn't. I did what I did when I was in radio – I pictured myself talking to a small roomful of friends. The presentation went without a hitch. I delivered the info and the people seemed to have liked it. We opened the floor to questions from the audience and the three of us fielded them flawlessly. Then, came the close. This part I was a little nervous about, but that was for nothing. We made over 300 sales that amounted to over $60,000. The next day, James sent a link to his list to watch the replay. That email generated another $30,000 in sales.

I decided that I liked webinars.

James knew that I did not know many people in the Internet marketing niche, so he asked if he could promote me on the "webinar circuit". The following week, he was holding a live conference in Las Vegas with his group of colleagues and asked me to fly down for some introductions. There, I met Jason Fladlien, Rachel Rofe', Brian Johnson, Tim Castleman, Wil Mattos, and John Rhodes. These were guys that were crushing it online with business to business (B2B) related eBooks and software. We gathered in James' suite at the Tuscany Casino. James ordered a few pizzas and I gave a live demonstration on how my Google News method worked. They were all super impressed. These were the masters of the Internet, as far as I was concerned, so impressing them was very exciting. Each of them set up dates with James for me to present the webinar to their respective audiences. As the broker of the deals, James would get a percentage of all sales made on those webinars. That's three ways I learned you could make money with webinars: hosting them, presenting them, and pimping them out.

CHAPTER 15

BECOMING A BIG FISH IN A SMALL POND

For the next several weeks, I spent most nights doing my presentation for various marketers. James continued to pimp me out to all of his marketing friends. We made good money, so it was a win-win situation for everybody

While doing these webinars, I kept my eye on the goal, which was to sell more and more of my product. One thing I did not consider was the amount of exposure I was getting. I was "performing" in front of an audience of several hundred, each night. Even those that didn't buy were getting a good educational presentation. This hit me when I was going through a week's worth of emails. There were dozens of emails from people thanking me for the webinar presentation. Some people mentioned how refreshing it was to learn about something new, while others said they had been searching high and low for information about Google News. I showed my wife some of the thank you letters. She said, "Those aren't thank you letters, they are fan letters." Fan letters. Hmmm, I could get used to that.

One day, out of the blue, I received a call from a woman who said she worked with Brad Fallon at StomperNet. I had heard about StomperNet. It was a very expensive to join community where they taught people how to promote and market products or businesses online. Their annual live conference in Las Vegas was coming up and the woman said she wanted me to be one of the keynote speakers. She had attended one of my webinars and was impressed by my presentation and the content. I was blown away. My dream of speaking in front of a large audience was about to come true. Sure, I had a radio show, but I never had the chance to see the faces of any of the people I was talking to. This was a real auditorium in front of people that have flown from all over to see me. OK, there were others speaking, too, but I like to think they came to see me.

James flew in to support me. He introduced me to a lot of people he knew that were also there. I was making contacts. I was getting well known. I was nervous as hell.

Then, my time to take the stage came. Suddenly, the fear went away. I looked out into the audience of about 200 and it was like I got high. This was the drug I was looking for my entire life. My stage presentation was similar to my webinar presentation. I had done it so many times before that I knew it like the back of my hand. I nailed it. When it was over, I was mobbed by a small crowd. They wanted more info about Google News. This was incredibly exciting. Although he was probably exaggerating to be nice, James said I was born to be on stage.

I was 37 years old and it had been a few months since I realized I was not going to be a starting pitcher for the Boston Red Sox. Eddie wasn't calling to ask if I would be the new lead singer of Van Halen, either. It was time to find a new dream that would fill my look-at-me personality, only this wasn't a dream. This was becoming a reality.

As the weeks went on, the mail kept coming in. I was becoming more and more known in this industry. I was becoming a player. I didn't care that I was only a big fish in a small pond, I liked the attention, until that attention started to go negative.

I set up a Google Alert for my name. That is a feature Google offers that will send you an email every time a specified keyword is mentioned in a new page spidered by the search engine. One morning, Google sent me an email alerting me about a new blog post that included my name. It was written by a guy named Marc Harty. Marc spent a bunch of time breaking down the webinars that I was presenting. In short, he was saying that my presentation was full of shit.

Marc mentioned the claims I made in my presentations and then offered his "reality check", which, of course, was the opposite of what I was saying. For example, he alluded that I talked about how easy it was to create a site that would be approved for Google News. He then broke down how much work was involved. The real reality check is that I never mentioned creating a news site was easy. In fact, I repeatedly told my audiences this is a real business opportunity that must be taken seriously and only somebody that was willing to commit to the time and work investment should consider purchasing my program. I liked telling people this. I felt it separated me from the guru types that were telling people they had the solution easy riches. But, people like Marc are used to promoting those guru types and fueling the illusions of his readers that making money online is fast and simple.

Marc went on to say that my claims of getting approved as a Google News publisher in a couple of weeks were bogus. He posted quotes from a guy who knew a guy that got approved, but it took him two years. I contacted Marc, asking him if he had actually seen my course and read about the ways I taught people to shorten the process. He had not. I offered to give him a tour of the course, so that he would be informed and either rewrite or remove the article. He was not interested. I asked if he would like to interview me and edit the articles, once he had more accurate information. He said no.

Meanwhile, the chat forum on my site was being filled with posts from happy customers that were getting approved, one after another. I sent screenshots of these posts to Marc. He did not respond.

Marc's article was the first of a few naysayers to emerge. My next Google Alert pointed me to a thread in the Google News Publisher Forum, hosted by Google itself. This was a support forum where news approved publishers could get questions answered about the news program. It seems they were a bit upset that the secret was out. When I wrote Google Red Carpet, there were approximately 25,000 Google News publishers in existence. This may sound like a lot, but competing for rank against 25,000 is nothing compared to the hundreds of millions of competitors "normal" web publishers have to compete against for rank. The Google News publishers were angry about the slew of new sites entering their sacred playing field. I was called every name in the book. Some called me a scammer for teaching my methods. One person said I should be arrested and thrown in jail. Seriously?

That thread and Marc's articles became fodder for even more libelous material being published about me. One guy, named Bill Davis, made a blog post about me, citing Marc's website as his source. There was a picture of a pile of shit, the caption read, "E. Brian Rose". I offered this guy a tour of my course. He, too, had no interest in actually seeing the product he was writing a review about. I later saw him at a live conference and confronted him. He was told by several people there that my course was legit and agreed to take his post down. Eight months later, I had to remind him of his promise. He eventually removed it.

This was really getting to me. My course was genuine. It gave real tips on how to write news articles, source your information, conduct interviews, and monetize what you publish on the Internet. This information has many good applications, even outside the realm of Google News. As for the tips on how to get approved by Google, almost all of that was compiled from Google's emails to me and information published to the web by Google itself. As proud as I was to see so many people benefiting from my course, the bad press was really getting me down.

I suspended sales and stopped doing the webinars. I wanted to spend my time combating the misinformation being spread about me. I asked my students to reply to these articles and forum posts, explaining the positive results they were having. For a while, it seemed to have worked, but the naysayers were relentless. They did not stop until their agenda was addressed by Google. Google addressed it alright. They temporarily stopped approving sites to their Google News program. This sucked for me and, most of all, for my students.

I spent the next few weeks researching new content to add to my course. Google News was not the only way to monetize the craft that I was teaching. I added a bunch of new lessons and ended the monthly fees people were having to pay to access the material. I even went as far as offering a full refund for anyone that wanted one. Only six people took me up on that offer.

Eventually, Google began accepting sites again, only with a bit more stringent rules. I updated the course to reflect these new rules. Then, the email I didn't want to get came in. A representative of Google News contacted me. He told me that some of my students were abusing the news system. He pointed out several sites, made by students of Google Red Carpet, that started off with great content, only to eventually start posting spammy advertisements to their sites. Google News is an automatic aggregator. There are no humans that check what you write, so the spam articles were being indexed and displayed prominently, just like legitimate news. I assured him that I didn't teach this kind of publishing and made it clear to him that, in my course, high quality original material is the only kind of content that would keep them in the good graces of Google. He wasn't impressed with my rebuttal. The result was all of my own personal news sites were delisted from the Google News program. Several of my students' sites were also delisted. I was asked to never apply again.

My course is still available and still contains relevant information and instruction on creating a news site, generating content, and monetizing. The difference is, now I give it away for free at gredcarpet.com.

Despite the fact that my course is now free, Marc Harty refuses to remove the ridiculous blog post he made about my product. He is, apparently, enjoying all the free traffic he gets when people search for my name on Google. Some people just don't have a nice bone in their body.

CHAPTER 16

LEARNING TO SPEAK

When I was a teenager, I realized I wanted to do something big in life. I didn't want to be ordinary. I wanted to make a lot of money and I wanted people to know who I was. I started watching the news and the new 24 hour cable news channels. I saw the talking heads and wanted to be one of them.

While in Somalia, the Army had a makeshift radio station for the deployed troops. It played mainly music, but at night, there was a show that combined talk and music. The guy that hosted it was hilarious. He was controversial. I can't remember his name, but he reminded me of Robin Williams in the movie *"Good Morning, Vietnam"*.

My job as a combat video producer gave me the opportunity to get to places normal troops had no access to. When I heard this voice on the radio, I knew I had to meet him. I scheduled an interview and headed to the station with my gear. As I watched him speak into the microphone, I recalled my teenage years when I dreamed of being heard.

After the interview, I asked the guy if I could give it a shot. I wanted to see if I had what it took to be on the radio. He told me he could sneak me on, but it would have to be somewhere around three in the morning. I didn't care. I just wanted to try it.

I set my alarm for 2 a.m. and started walking. Half way there, I noticed a pack of stray dogs heading towards me. Next thing I knew, they were surrounding me. They were nasty little dogs, about the size of beagles, all covered in mange. It may sound silly to be scared of these tiny mutts, but one bite could mean a series of rabies shots, so I was a bit concerned. As they came closer, I chambered a round in my nine millimeter Beretta. This was a bad situation. I could easily fire a shot and scare the dogs away, but I was close to the outer wall of the compound and the wall was being guarded by Pakistani forces. They would hear the shot, fire at me, and ask questions later. My choices seemed slim, I could get eaten by tiny wild dogs or get blown away by Pakistanis. Fortunately, a Blackhawk helicopter came in for a landing at that very moment and frightened the dogs away.

On to the radio station.

When I walked in, my guy was there waiting. He said I could have thirty minutes on the air. He set up a tape recorder that would automatically start recording when I switched the microphone on. As my first song ended, I read a card that had the day's weather report on it and introduced the next song. The thirty minutes seemed to fly by. I loved it and thought I did great. After my "shift", I was handed my air check tape. I asked how I did. He said, "Well, you did."

When I got back to my tent, I popped the cassette into my big yellow Sony Walkman and listened.

Awful.

I sounded like a punk kid from Boston. This was the first time I realized how bad my accent was. I didn't sound anything like the people I heard on the radio and TV. If I was going to be heard, and I mean really heard, then I had to learn to speak properly.

I made it a personal goal to lose my accent. I went to the library and checked out books on speaking skills. I practiced by reading everything out loud, concentrating on annunciating every word, even those pesky R's that us Bostonians like to pretend don't exist. Pretty soon, I was starting to sound like a respectable human being. I went from "pahkin' the cah in Hahvahd Yahd" to "Parking the car in Harvard Yard".

If I had to look back and think of the one decision I made that has had the biggest impact on my life, it was the decision to learn to speak. I used this skill in so many ways to accomplish my goals. I became a radio disc jockey. I hosted a television show. I presented webinars. I gave speeches on stage. I made sales. None of these things would have been successful if I had not learned to speak.

Learning to speak is not just for guys with big egos that have the need to be on TV. It is a skill that all entrepreneurs should learn.

If you take my advice just one time, make this that piece of advice: Learn to speak to a crowd. Whether the crowd is in front of you, watching you on video, or even a webinar, you need to know how to address groups of people. This is a talent you can teach yourself and one that will stay with you for the rest of your life.

No matter where your life takes you, if you can speak in front of a crowd, you will go farther than the people who cannot. Being able to get your message across to a group of people is one of the most powerful weapons a person can have in their career arsenal.

If you can convey your message in a clear and concise way, people will listen to you and once you have the knack for getting a person's true attention, the world is your oyster.

For some of you, the mere idea of speaking in front of a crowd makes you shiver, but it is a fear that you can easily get over. It's actually pretty easy. All you need are a few key things.

Know your content – There is nothing worse than when somebody gives a speech on a topic they are not completely read up on. The more you know about your topic, the more confident you will be as a speaker. Whether you are speaking in front of an audience of three or three hundred, the crowd will sense it if you are winging it. Do your homework and know your material.

Practice, but don't over practice – Practice your entire presentation several times, out loud. After a few runs, record yourself. As you play it back, take notes on areas you feel need improvements. Make the necessary changes and record yourself again. Repeat these steps until you feel you have nailed it, then stop. Some people make the mistake of over rehearsing and over editing their copy. The most important thing is that your presentation makes sense and conveys your message.

Don't be monotone – If you do not speak with enthusiasm, your audience will not be enthused. Make your voice fluctuate. Let the audience know how passionate you are about your topic. When you are excited about a certain part, make sure it comes across in your voice. "Ask not what you country can do for you" would just be a side note if JFK had said it in monotone!

"Ask" for applause – Take a few minutes to search for some State of the Union Addresses on YouTube. The media always counts the number of applause breaks in those speeches, so the Presidents purposely incorporate them into their speeches. Take notice of how they use the speed of their wording, emphasis on words or phrases, and dramatic pauses right before the Congress breaks out into applause. It's as if they are asking the audience to start clapping. If you can perfect this, you will have applause on demand.

Eliminate the Ums – Saying "um" is a common replacement for words when you don't know what to say. This is a no-no in public speaking. Instead of saying "um" when searching for words, repeat your last sentence or simply say nothing. That pause gives you a moment to come up with your next words and gives the audience a chance to let the last thing you said sink in. It takes a bit of practice, but once you nail this, you will be well on your way to becoming a professional speaker. Most people say "um" hundreds of times a day. Practice eliminating it from your everyday speech and it will be much easier to eliminate it when speaking in front of a crowd.

Get to know your audience – If you are speaking from a stage, you should make an effort to mingle with the folks you are going to be speaking to, before you go on. Familiarity will give you confidence. Make an extra effort to seek out the people sitting in the first few rows. If you get to know those people, you can focus on them while speaking and it will seem more like you are talking to a friend. If possible, try and get people you already know to sit close to the stage. This way, you can look to them and not feel like you are in front of a group of strangers.

Use personal stories – The audience is far more likely to relate to your talk if you incorporate a personal touch. Make them realize how your topic can affect a real person, namely you. It allows them to get a glimpse of who they are listening to, making you more of a human being, than just some public speaker.

Join Toastmasters – If you are serious about learning to be a better public speaker, then Toastmasters is a club for you. There are chapters all over the world and anybody can join. Toastmasters is a club filled with people who want to be better communicators and mentors that help people achieve that goal. In addition to learning great speaking skills, you will also be networking with other like-minded individuals and that is never a bad thing.

CHAPTER 17

CALL ME THE KING

Despite the bad press I had gotten from a few blog posts and forum threads, the good things being written about me were outweighing the bad. Between the eBook and the membership site, I had thousands of customers who were pleased with my teaching. I started a blog and began to write articles. I also emailed my list of customers a bi-weekly newsletter filled with tips and tricks I had learned along the way.

I have been doing business online for many years and had learned a lot of lessons. I figured I still had a fresh perspective on things and there were people that really wanted to know what I know. The "info product" industry, as it is called, was seeing fast growth. I read that over a billion dollars a year in eBooks and video courses were being sold online. I started to think this might be a good future for me.

I went through my saved emails, looking through some of the praise I received from my first two products. I wanted to see if anything jumped out at me that I could teach in more detail. Then, I read one email where the guy went on and on about how much he enjoyed one of the webinars he attended. The light bulb flicked on. Webinars were starting to sprout up left and right and I was fresh off a "webinar tour" that people seemed to have really liked. I was confident I could create a workshop that broke down how to profit from webinars.

I began by jotting down some bullet points of the topics I wanted to cover. I came up with a couple dozen. Then, it dawned on me: What better way to teach a webinar course than with an actual webinar? This also cut my production time down. Instead of having to write thousands of words and publish an eBook, I could now just make a PowerPoint presentation and present to a live audience. I could sell admission to the live event for a premium and, later, sell the recordings at a discounted price.

I got started right away. I created slides with bullet points of topics I knew I could ramble on about. This took just a couple of hours. Like my first info product, the plan was to sell this on the Warrior Forum, so my next step was to write up the sales copy for the WSO post. I contacted some of the pros and gurus that hosted my webinars and asked them for some testimonials. These testimonials became the bulk of my sales letter on the forum.

Brad Gosse wrote, *"I can't imagine getting trained to run webinars by anyone else. You are a fool to pass this up. EBR knows how to make it rain."*

Mike Cowles wrote, *"If you do anything this year, buy this WSO! Why would I say something so strong? Because I did and after only 90 minutes with EBR on the phone, I generated over $6,000!"*

Ron Douglas wrote, *"Thanks to the tips he gave me, my webinar for VideoForward.com now consistently converts at over 35%."*

These are strong statements. It is social proof from some well-known people in the industry. Whenever you launch a product, always seek out testimonials from known people in the industry you are marketing to. It doesn't matter if you are selling an eBook on how to get social security, how to choose what plastic surgery to get, or how to train a dog. Always seek out quotes from experts in the field and use them in your sales copy. They are not going to come to you, so you have to ask. Ask everybody. The worst they can say is no.

I recalled my conversation with Wayne Allyn Root. The one where he told me to call myself what I wanted people to call me and they will, in turn, call me that. At the top of the sales page was a headline that read, "Learn How to Crush Webinars from 'The King of Webinars', E. Brian Rose".

The rest of my sales copy explained the training that I would be giving and the date and time of the live webinar. I charged $97, which was a lot higher than the average prices of WSOs currently for sale.

By now, the Warrior Plus system that I previously used to track my sales had evolved. It was now known as an "affiliate network". Other users could now promote my products for a commission. I created some sample emails and gave it out to all of my colleagues. We call this "swipe copy". The swipe copy gave details of the training and, of course, referred to me as "The King of Webinars". Soon, dozens of marketers were emailing their lists a message about my course and spreading the word that I was "the king". Call yourself what you want people to call you. Thanks again for that one, Wayne.

I sold 136 virtual tickets to my live training session. At $97 a pop, I generated over $13,000 in sales. The training went off without a hitch. I allowed questions from the audience and answered them all. A few months later, I opened up sales for the recordings, selling the training as an on demand video training course. The audience Q and A session became a selling point in the updated sales copy. Another 336 sales were made from the recordings.

CHAPTER 18

GOOD LUCK WITH THAT

The folks on my email list really seemed to dig me and the content I was sharing with them. One of the things I think they liked about me was that I was no nonsense. I would tell it like it is and not try and stroke them. If the industry was buzzing about a particular product or guru, I would give my honest opinion on it. Sometimes, the hot product or person of the week is nothing more than a bunch of bullshit.

It was a common misconception that the best way to make money online was to create info products that teach others how to make money online. Many guru types taught this as the rule and lots of newbies bought right into it. This is absurd for a number of reasons. First, who wants to learn how to make money online from somebody that is just learning how to make money online? Second, marketing to other marketers is like being a magician and performing in front of an audience full of other magicians. They know your tricks. Every type of sales technique you will use, they have seen before and are expecting it. You don't get the same type of know it all audience when you venture outside the world of fellow marketers and wannabe marketers.

The advice I gave to my followers was to create and market products in a niche that you were passionate about. If you are a hard core exercise enthusiast, then that is what you should build your online business around. If you love arts and crafts, write a series of how-to eBooks. Create a blog and write about it. Build an audience that you can market to. Do all of those things, but be sure you do it with a niche you care about. Do what you like and you will not get burned out. Building a successful online business means you will constantly be immersing yourself in whatever niche you choose to market in. The last thing you want is to spend your days schmoozing in chat forums about a topic you hate. Marketing online can be very fun, but not if you are marketing products that bore you.

This type of advice went against the grain. This is not what they were used to hearing, but it made sense and they wanted to hear more. They were digging me and when consumers dig you, you need to give them what they want, which is more content and more things to buy. More info products were on the way. I would create and sell them to my followers, but I also wanted to use these products to expand my list of customers. The best way to do that is to recruit affiliates to market for me.

I wanted to recruit as many affiliate partners as I could for these products, but I didn't feel right about cold calling random marketers and asking them to promote me. Instead, I promoted their products to my list, first. Then, after I made a few sales for them, I was on their radar. This was an ice breaker for when I called on them to promote for me. My list was very responsive and they ended up buying quite a few of the products I was endorsing. This also earned me some nice commissions.

I wrote a series of short reports. Some were about how I built a solid relationship with my email list, some were about my days as a dropship marketer, and some were about creating videos for the web. They all sold very well. The reports were priced low enough to where they were affordable to aspiring marketers, usually around $7. I wasn't getting rich off of these, but I was adding more and more paying customers to my email list, which meant more money could be made by promoting other marketer's products.

The more I used the Warrior Plus system for selling my products and affiliate products, the more I wished it had more features. For example, it would have been nice to have the ability to offer automatically delivered bonuses for the products I was promoting. When a product launched on the system, many different affiliates would mail their lists promoting it. The community was not that large, so a lot of people on these different lists overlapped. They would often get emails from multiple marketers, all promoting the same product. I thought it would be a great idea to have the ability to say, "If you buy this product from the link in my email, you will also automatically receive my new report on such and such." This seemed like a great way to allow the more savvy marketers to get a leg up on their competition.

Another feature that sounded nice was the ability to create sales funnels. A sales funnel is the process of leading your customers and prospective customers. For example, once they buy a short report, they are directed to another related offer. This new offer might be an upgraded version of something they just bought or simply a product that compliments the original purchase. The funnel could also have downsells. If they say no to one offer, they are directed to a different offer, usually with a lower price tag. Sales funnels can also be used for pre-selling a prospective buyer. They sign up to receive a free eBook and a series of emails follows, pitching them to buy a related item. I wanted to see affiliates be able to mail for one item and be credited with commissions for any item throughout the funnel.

> *(If you think this is all new to you, I assure you it's not. Sales funnels are actually all around you. When you go to McDonalds and order a burger, they upsell you by asking if you want fries with that. Buy a car and you'll get upsell pitches for a better stereo system, leather seats, or an extended warranty. These upsells are all part of a sales funnel.)*

I wanted to be able to use Warrior Plus on offers outside the Warrior Forum, like on my own websites.

I wanted to have the ability to recruit affiliates for webinars.

I wanted affiliates to get paid on every sale they made, not just every other sale (at the time, affiliates only got money for every other sale made).

I wanted a lot of things and I wrote them all down.

Meanwhile, being the self-crowned king of webinars was leading to more opportunities. I was asked to give some tips on stage at an upcoming Internet marketing conference and, of course, I was happy to do it. The more exposure the better.

I spun this well, announcing to my email list that I was chosen as a featured speaker. The goal, of course, was to lend even more credibility to myself, which leads to selling more of my products and the products I was recommending.

Live conferences are fantastic and I was really looking forward to this one. You can usually learn a lot from the speakers presenting at these conferences, but the interactions and business relationships you make in the lobbies and hotel bars are what is most valuable.

It was at this event that I met some of the people in marketing that I admired. I also scheduled several people to present webinars to my list. James Jones had been pushing me to host a weekly webinar for marketers. Times were very different back then. Not a lot of folks were hosting webinars. James said, "You should do Friday nights. Nobody is doing Friday night webinars." Compare that to today, when you can find upwards of ten webinars a day going off, any day of the week.

Mike Lantz, owner of Warrior Plus, was there, too. We immediately hit it off. He was a really nice guy and I genuinely liked him. On the final day of the event, most people had early morning flights out, but he and I were scheduled to fly later in the afternoon. President Obama made a surprise visit to the city, causing the airport to shut down. We were both stranded in Raleigh a few extra hours. This was actually perfect. I wanted to share with him my ideas of how Warrior Plus could be better.

I gave my spiel and Mike listened intently. He acknowledged that all of these things were good ideas and that he had already thought of most of them. However, he also said that he was content with the way things were. I could almost understand his thinking. Being the only rodeo in town, you don't really have to improve things. I asked him if he would still feel that way if another site were to pop up and compete against him. He said, "Why, are you planning on starting one?" I don't know why I answered yes, but I did. He humbly said, "That would be great. Good luck with that," but I knew what he really meant. He meant, "Ya right! Never gonna happen!"

On the flight home, I started thinking about what it would take if I actually did consider creating a site that competed against Warrior Plus. I knew nothing about coding a website to do all of these things, so at the very least, I would need to hire a programmer. I grabbed my laptop from the overhead bin and started making some notes. I made two lists. One list included everything I would want to see in an affiliate network site from the viewpoint of an affiliate. The other, everything from the viewpoint of a creator of products and seller. By the time the flight attendant made the announcement to turn off all electronics, I had a pretty good outline for what I considered to be the dream site for online marketing. But, that's all it was. When I got home, I went on with my life.

CHAPTER 19

MASTERMINDING FOR PROFIT

I made sure I kept in touch with some of the folks I met at the event. Creating solid business relationships with smart and able people is a must to succeed as an entrepreneur. It's also the thing that scares some people the most. Many think you can choose a career working from home to avoid talking to others. Maybe you can, but it is always easier to have allies – people you can lean on and can lean on you, people that can help you and you help them. These are also the people that you can go to when you have a great idea. They may have resources that you don't have or ideas to add to the mix. Relationships are important in life and in business. If you are shy or not good dealing with people, then you should work to overcome this, immediately. Being a successful entrepreneur often requires you to step outside of your comfort zones.

A few of the folks I met and hung out with at the event seemed to have some good synergy and we started a private Skype room. That's a chat room that you can create, within the Skype chat software, that was only available to us. We started it to share concepts and bounce ideas off one another.

The room consisted of Brad Gosse, Ron Douglas, Bryan Zimmerman, Mike Carraway, and myself. Brad had quite a bit of notoriety in the online business world. He had made a fortune years before promoting online porn sites. Ron was a New York Times bestselling author. He had written a cookbook called *"America's Most Wanted Recipes"* and been featured on all the morning talk shows. All of us were now doing similar things online. We were creating info products and each had a growing audience. It was great to surround myself with smart, positive energy guys, like these. They all shared my type of sense of humor, too. It was great to break up the day with the occasional funny message. Working from home can be very lonely at times. Having a group of friends that share your vision and can support you is essential.

We started to think of ways to combine our efforts and expand our individual reaches or even possibly working together on a joint venture. Eventually, we decided on creating a membership site called JV Mastermind Network or JVMN for short. It would be a site where people paid a monthly fee to get a live daily training session with one of the mentors.

There were currently five of us, so we needed to add two more to the list, so we could schedule ourselves for one training day a week. Jeremy Kelsall was a WordPress plugin developer that had been putting out some interesting products. We all liked him and he was a good fit. For the last spot, we wanted to find a female. Mike suggested a woman named Holly Cotter. I didn't know Holly, but her name sounded familiar. After Googling her, I found that she had some well received info products in the space we were all working in. I did not find anything negative, so she got my vote.

We all had a conference call on GoToMeeting.com and brainstormed how we were going to launch and promote the new site. Holly and I butted heads from the get go. It seemed like she would try to one up every idea I would put out there. It was almost as if she had it out for me from the start. For some reason, I was feeling the same. I just didn't like her, but we managed to put our differences aside and we moved on.

The site launched with all of us emailing our lists an invitation to a webinar. During the webinar, we each had five minutes to dish out our best Internet marketing tip. Then, we presented the offer to join our mastermind group and get these kind of tips every day. The webinar, which had about 800 people on it, resulted in a couple of hundred sales. More subscribers were added with follow up emails we all sent to our list.

The kickoff went well, my initial live training session was a crash course on creating presentations for webinars. Bryan showed people how to make the most out of your mailing list. Ron talked about using viral marketing. All of the presentations were top notch, recorded in front of a live audience and archived for members to watch on demand. Every couple of weeks, we recorded a group chat, where we all spoke openly about what projects we were working on. The paid subscribers loved it. They were getting valuable lessons and we were getting more and more fans.

One month, we hosted an online "shark tank" event. It was similar to the TV show where successful entrepreneurs listen to pitches from folks with inventions or business ideas they need funding or partnerships for. We promoted the event a few weeks in advance and picked some finalists from the many applications we received. The ones we picked got ten minutes to present to us. This took place in front of a live audience on a webinar. The winner had some really cool software that stored and indexed content that came with private label rights. That's pre-written articles and eBooks that you could edit and claim authorship of. His prize was having the product marketed to the lists of the JVMN mentors.

I only presented one day a week on JVMN, so I still had plenty of time to work on my solo projects. I began writing a course that I eventually called EBR Gameplan. It was the actual blueprint I used to get started in the info product business, complete with step by step instructions for creating info products and marketing them. I turned the content into another membership site, where people paid a monthly fee for continued access and new content that was released monthly.

I love the membership model, because you only have to sell a customer one time, but continue getting paid, month after month. This is true passive income. The various membership plugins for WordPress made it easy to "drip feed" content to members. You create it and the system would automatically drip the content to your members as specified intervals. In my case, new content would drip out each month. Months or even years of income from work that was done one time - that's called passive income and it is awesome!

The turmoil between Holly and me continued. In our weekly conference calls and in the Skype room, we argued like siblings. Something about her just bugged me.

Bryan and I started hosting webinars together. He told me that he had booked Holly to present to our audience. I rolled my eyes, but went with the flow. We mailed our lists and had a pretty substantial sized audience. Holly's presentation was about creating apps for mobile phones. At the end of the presentation, she made the audience an offer for some service or software that created these apps. She went on and on about how profitable this business opportunity was.

As the host of the webinar, my job was to make positive reinforcement statements that push the viewers towards buying, but I felt it was also my job to ask tough questions. I had a gut feeling that Holly's hype about how much money could be made was based on theory and not actual results. I knew if I asked the question it would mean we would not make any money off of this webinar, but I felt like I had to do it. "Holly, how much have you personally made off of these apps?" She stuttered through her answer, eventually saying that she has not made any money. "So, it is all theory," I followed up with. She was hesitant to agree, but did. "All right, there you have it, guys. Click here to buy." Two out of the hundreds in attendance bought. Bryan called me after the webinar. I thought he was going to be upset about the amount of money I cost us, but he was glad I asked the question. So were the viewers. I received a lot of emails from people that were appreciative I didn't just push them into buy something without revealing the whole story.

Holly got her revenge, later on. She scheduled me to present a webinar for her audience. She was supposed to be promoting it for a couple of days. When the two-hour webinar was scheduled to start, there were three people in attendance, so she decided to cancel. Holly then sent an email to her entire list, saying the webinar was cancelled due to my refusing to present to so few people. Jerk.

It was shortly after that I realized why I had such a bad taste in my mouth about Holly. I guess it was subliminal. I went back to the blog that trashed my Google Red Carpet product the previous year. Low and behold, a comment was made by Holly. She wrote:

> *"Marc, I appreciate you exposing the inconsistencies and fallacies of the "Google Red Carpet" tactic so clearly. It's getting more and more difficult for consumers to discern a good product (one that teaches a solid strategy) from a bad one... with so many "experts" promoting junk products these days."*

She was oh so grateful for someone exposing how evil I am, with all of my "inconsistencies and fallacies", but the moment she was presented with a money-making opportunity to partner with me, she took it. There's nothing I hate more than somebody that jumps from bandwagon to bandwagon.

Holly and I don't do business together, anymore. In fact, she was eventually kicked out of JVMN for lack of participation. I haven't seen her name come up in any circles, since then.

CHAPTER 20

SHARING SECRETS

On a more positive note…

I was thinking more and more about my talk with Mike Lantz and the outline I created on that flight home. Was it really possible for me to create an affiliate network that included everything I thought would be needed for affiliates and vendors? I was starting to think it was.

After a few days of trying to talk myself out of jumping into a project of this size, I said screw it and started making some phone calls. I was going through a list of programmers I found online, hoping to find one that could share the vision and want to partner with me. I had some money, but I didn't think I had the money it would take to flat out hire a team of coders to take on such a project. Also, the thought of a contracted coder just handing me a finished product and walking away did not sit well with me. What if something broke? What if he went out of business and I needed something tweaked? These were important things I needed to consider. The ideal situation was to find a coder to partner with.

So, I called. And I called. And I called.

One thing I learned, there are people that build things and there are people that market those things. Coders build things and very rarely do they see the potential in marketing things. In short, nobody wanted to partner with me. They all wanted money up front and to hand over the finished product when they were done. Some firms quoted as little as $50,000 to do the job, others quoted as high as $200,000.

I kept searching, but on the down low. I made everybody I talked with sign a nondisclosure agreement, before I sent them my spec sheet. I didn't want word to get out that I was looking to do this. Not so much because I thought somebody would beat me to the punch, but more for fear of being laughed at. This was a big project and most people look at big projects as being impossible. I wasn't one of those.

So, I kept quiet and continued doing my thing. I did my weekly training session with the JV Mastermind Network, I hosted webinars, and I busted out more eBooks and short reports. The train was moving along, but I knew in the back of my mind the ideas I had for a new affiliate network would be such an asset for the industry, not to mention make a huge amount of money for me.

After a couple of months searching and searching for somebody to code the darn thing, I was almost to the point of giving up. Maybe that "ya right" look I got from Mike Lantz was legit. Maybe this was a mission impossible.

Bryan Zimmerman called to chat about the JV Mastermind site and we got to talking about some ideas we had for future info products. He mentioned a feature that he wished Warrior Plus had. I can't remember what it was, but it was something I hadn't thought of yet. I said what the fuck and started blabbing about my ideas for a totally new network. I told him all the ideas of the new features and the trouble I was having finding somebody to code it for me. I expected to hear laughter, but Bryan said, "Let's get Chad Casselman on the phone. I think he can do this."

Bryan said I met Chad at the last marketing conference, but I couldn't quite place him. Then, he reminded me that Chad was also the guy who won the JVMN shark tank event. I had no idea this guy had the skills to take on such a large project.

The three of us got on a conference call. I bared all. I told them my vision of what features the site should have and some kick ass plans I had for marketing it. Bryan had some vision of his own, adding even more ideas to the table. Then Chad spoke. In an incredibly laid back voice, he said, "If you guys think it can work, I can do it." This was a bit concerning. We were talking about a venture that could potentially bring in millions of dollars, not to mention put our reputations on the line. How could he be so nonchalant about it?

Zim, as we began to call Bryan, and I then talked privately. I expressed my concerns about Chad being so casual. He said, when you've got the gift, you can be casual. He then told me about Chad's qualifications. Chad used to work for one of those big programming firms, much like the ones that quoted me hundreds of thousands of dollars to complete my project. He was currently building out software for Jason Fladlien and Wil Mattos, two extremely successful marketers. Oh and he was a college professor, teaching computer programming classes.

OK, Chad is qualified.

I had another idea I wanted to share with the group. This time, it was an affiliate network specifically made for webinars. Normally, when somebody had a webinar to present, they would partner up with a marketer who had a following and the marketer would invite their followers to the webinar presentation. This left everybody that didn't have a big marketing list out in the cold. I had an idea to create a marketplace where vendors could list a presentation day and time and multiple affiliates could mail their lists for the same webinar. This would help the vendor attract bigger crowds by having more than just one marketer mail out invites and affiliates with smaller lists could participate in lucrative webinar commissions that they would normally have missed out on.

The guys loved the idea. Chad said he could build that system in less than two months and the code he created for it would be the backbone of the main affiliate network.

Like clockwork, Chad delivered, just as he said he would. Roughly two months after the initial conversation, the three of us launched a site called WebinarSwaps. The timing was perfect, too. There was an Internet marketing conference coming up and we were given permission to announce the site's launch from the main stage. We also emailed all of our own personal marketing lists, letting our customers know about the site.

Four hundred people signed up on the first day. Soon, there were over a thousand.

We scheduled a bunch of webinars to run bi-weekly. Zim and I acted as co-hosts for each. The first webinar had over 800 attendees and generated thousands of dollars for the presenter, the affiliates, and our new company. WebinarSwaps made money by taking a small percentage from every sale made through the webinars. We also acted as an affiliate, getting a full commission, usually 50%, for any attendees we invited that showed up and made a purchase.

Things were rockin' and rollin', but I couldn't wait for the main event to kick off. The affiliate network that was going to change the way people do business online. Yes, I was that confident.

CHAPTER 21

LAUNCHING WITH CONTROVERSY

When the three of us made the deal to become partners, Zim and I thought it would be best if Chad was exclusive to the company and no longer did side work for anybody else. Knowing this was a big portion of his income, we told him to keep doing it until we had proved to him that we can make money roll in. After several months of WebinarSwaps kicking butt, we mentioned to Chad it might be that time. We knew this would be hard for him, but Chad stuck to his word.

Up until that time, he had still been making software for Jason Fladlien and Wil Mattos and they were not ready to let Chad go without a fight. The two made him a very lucrative offer to work for them exclusively. Chad turned it down.

We were now weeks away from beta testing the new site and we had yet to come up with a name. Zim and I brainstormed until we had a list of names, but most of the names we came up with weren't available as a dot com. I couldn't remember which one of us came up with the name JVZoo, but during one of our media interviews, Zim did credit it to me. I'll take it.

The "JV" in JVZoo stands for joint venture, a term used in business that basically means to partner. In the online marketing world, your affiliates are often referred to as "JV partners".

I went back to my old playbook from the poker days and we put together an advisory board of people we would want the new site to be associated with. We recruited Brad Gosse, Ben Littlefield, Dan Ardebili, Mike Carraway, and Brad Spencer. These were five guys that had a loyal following in the online marketing world. They were also smart guys we knew could help us come up with new ideas that would make the site better.

With beta testing so close, that meant the site launch was not far off – and that meant we need to have a good marketing plan.

We held off telling a lot of people about the upcoming site. There's nothing worse than entrepreneurs that say what they're "gonna do", so we kept it fairly quiet. No "guess what's coming" or "pre-signup now" type of advertising. We had to launch and had to launch with some sort of splash.

Controversy always brings in the curious minds and that was my plan for our launch. Earlier in the year, I had written a short eBook about a very controversial topic. I thought this might be the right fit for the first official product to launch on JVZoo. Like my Google News eBook, this was a topic that had yet to be broached in the Internet marketing world. Sure, people knew it existed, but most were afraid to put their name on it.

The topic was the General Public License, often referred to as the GPL. The GPL is a license agreement attached to many software products. It is an agreement that is commonly found in WordPress themes and plugins.

The GPL goes into specific detail as to what rights the holder of the software has. It is actually quite lenient as to what you can do with products that have adopted the license. For example, you are allowed to distribute verbatim copies of the software for free or you can charge a fee. You are also allowed to make changes to the software, as long as the new version continues to be licensed under the GPL. For this reason, many WordPress themes are actually derivatives of other WordPress themes licensed under the GPL.

In laymen's terms: many of the WordPress themes that companies charge upwards of several hundred dollars for actually have this lenient license. That means you can buy from one of these companies and then resell it to the masses for a lower price or even give it away for free, if you chose to.

Obviously, this is a "secret" these development companies wanted to keep on the down low. They didn't want a guy like me telling the masses that they can freely distribute software that is being sold for hundreds of dollars.

When I wrote the eBook, I knew it would be controversial. I knew it would bring out arguments from both sides. The developers would scream I am teaching an unethical practice that gives people a license to steal, while the common sense crowd would argue that license was given by the developers themselves. It was an explosive debate waiting to happen. To demonstrate the GPL in action, I planned to sell the eBook with a bonus of dozens of commercial WordPress themes that normally sell at the developers' websites for $79 to $129, each. This was sure to incite an even higher level of controversy. I told Zim this was the product we should use to officially launch JVZoo. He agreed.

I spent the next couple of weeks recruiting joint venture partners that would promote the eBook to their followers, email lists, and blog readers. I went through the list of folks I had hosted or presented webinars with. For many of them, this was the first they were hearing about the soon to be launched JVZoo affiliate network. They were excited to hear about the features. They were also excited to promote a product that contained a fresh topic for our industry.

Chad had been working behind the scenes with the members of our advisory board and a few other carefully selected marketers. They had been quietly testing every aspect of the site. When we got the green light from Chad and his team, we launched the eBook for sale on the Warrior Forum.

The affiliates mailed on cue and the people started coming. And they started buying. Then they started talking. Just as we expected, the controversy of the eBook took effect. Proponents from both sides began an ongoing debate on the Warrior Forum chat forum and also on blog sites, throughout the Internet. Sales came pouring in and affiliates were making good commission money.

The eBook was selling and that was a good thing, but JVZoo was the real star. The site handled the enormous traffic and simultaneous transactions like a champ. And, just as we had hoped, the launch of this eBook brought a lot of attention to this new platform to sell digital products. Soon, the eBook became a side story and JVZoo was getting all of the attention. Over two thousand people signed up for the site in the first week. Many started listing products on the network, immediately.

Using a controversial product to launch JVZoo brought us some much needed early attention, but it was not a marketing plan. It was more like a publicity stunt. In order to keep the momentum going, we were going to have to come up with something much better than a spicy eBook.

We didn't have a large enough budget to bust out a full advertising campaign, so we had to get creative. When you can't afford to get your brand out to the masses, you have to think outside the box. I came up with a way to use social media and let others do our bidding for us.

There was an Internet marketing conference coming up in a few weeks. We decided we were going to throw a killer party at the hotel, during the conference. We had a budget of around $4,000. That would cover the costs of the party room rental, a DJ, an Elvis impersonator, photographer, and a fully stocked open bar. We anticipated around 150 people to come to the party, but the party wasn't for them, per say. It was for the tens of thousands of people in our target market that didn't come to the event. We had a little trick up our sleeves.

Before being able to enter the party, we made everybody pose on a red carpet with two models dressed in sexy JVZoo attire. The backdrop was a step and repeat wall with the JVZoo logo plastered all over it. It's the same type of wall you see at press conferences with the company name tiled across it. We knew many of the people there and were friends with them on FaceBook. Those that we didn't know, we made sure to "friend" them at some point.

The day after the party, we uploaded all of the red carpet photos to FaceBook and tagged the names of the people in the pictures. This made the attendee's photos appear on their respective FaceBook walls and in the newsfeeds of their friends. And the comments came pouring in.

"You were at a red carpet event?"

"Wish I was there!"

"Looks like a blast."

And they went on and on. The party was not for the people that attended. It was for their friends. On the Internet, our small, $4,000 budget event looked like a Hollywood gathering and this made our company look larger than life. The best part was all the free advertising we got when those pictures were shared, made into cover photos, and even Tweeted all over the Net.

Mike Lantz, from Warrior Plus, was also at that conference. He came to our party and congratulated us on the launching of the site. As I said, Mike is a nice guy, so I am sure that he meant it.

We continued to throw parties at events, each getting better and better. In North Carolina, we turned a dinner hall into a full casino and gave away prizes. In Orlando, we threw an eighties costume party. Soon, the buzz was all over that JVZoo throws "the best parties", but, most importantly, pictures from the events went viral on the Internet, spreading our brand farther than any advertising could ever do.

JVZoo makes its money by taking a cut out of every sale. It doesn't cost anything for somebody to list a product on our site. They only pay the small fee when a sale is made. To make lots of money, we needed lots of products listed and lots of affiliates promoting those products. To attract both, we held a series of contests and reinvested our earnings to provide cash prizes for the most sales. This resulted in swarms of new signups, new sales, and new revenue for the company.

The initial marketing plans were a success, but only half the battle. Once you get the attention of your target market and they sign up, you have to keep them as customers. We did this by providing the best customer support we could possibly provide. We hired a support team to handle technical issues. We also started a FaceBook group and created a series of videos tutorials. When a customer has a question, we made sure it was answered. We were also on top of suggestions. We paid attention to the trends of what people were asking for and implemented the popular suggestions.

JVZoo was profitable from day one, but I have been here before. I have built companies only to watch them crumble. I have partnered with people only to see them eventually lose their minds. I was prepared for the worst. But none of that happened. Things just kept moving on strong. It was a bit surreal.

Perhaps it's the fact that Zim, Chad, and I live in three different states and don't see each other every second of the day that made the partnership work so well. Of course, we've had our growing pains and the occasional arguments about which direction to go in, but the three of us all have the best interest of the business in mind. This was a welcome change to the partnerships I was used to.

CHAPTER 22

COMPETITORS GONE WILD

When JVZoo was in its early stages of development, I received an email from a guy named Billy Runner. Billy was a fellow Internet marketer. My only dealing with him was a brief webinar that James had set up during the Google Red Carpet days.

Billy's email said that he and a partner, named Jason Edges, were putting together an affiliate platform. He said the site was going to launch in 12 to 14 days and asked if I would be willing to be a beta tester and list some of my products on the site. I quickly replied, telling him my partners and I were also in the process of putting together an affiliate network. I wished him luck, but declined his offer. He responded with, "Sounds awesome... good luck with yours as well. Great thing about this business is, there's room for them."

That exchange of emails occurred in August of 2011. JVZoo launched in November of that year. Billy's affiliate network site still had not opened its doors, despite the email saying it was launching in 12 to 14 days, months prior.

I received another email from him in May of 2012. It was quite amusing. At this point, JVZoo had been open for business for months and was experiencing rapid growth. Billy and Jason's site still had not launched. The email accused our team of having people that are collecting "info about some ideas me and Jason have" for their new system and that we were already implementing their ideas. He went on to warn us that their site will "own the IM market" and for us to "watch out."

The guys and I had a good laugh over this one. We were being accused of copying a site that was supposed to have launched almost a year ago, but did not. None of us personally knew Billy or his partner and had zero knowledge of their plans, other than what he had told me in that first email.

Zim advised me to ignore the email and I really wanted to, but I am way too immature and I just couldn't. I responded with:

> *You can't be serious. We have much better things to do with our time than have people "collecting info about some ideas" you and some guy named Jason have for a platform that has yet to launch. We have been open for almost eight months and have regularly been implementing new features. That will not stop anytime soon, but rest assured, none of our features are your ideas, nor will future ones be.*

I find it egotistical that you think your platform, which has yet to even be released, is the only source for ideas.

I will keep this nice email for reference of your IM domination, in case a problem should arise in the future.

I didn't hear from Billy again for another few weeks. When I saw I had another email from him, I couldn't wait to read it. Drama amuses me. I expected another rant and was excited to read it.

The email wasn't a rant. In fact, it was just the opposite. He wanted to create some sort of partnership. Billy had decided it would be a good idea if we shared the contact information of our customers with him and he would do the same in return. This is crazy on a number of different levels. First, it would be a gross violation of our privacy policy. Our customers would be less than thrilled if we were handing over their email addresses to other companies. Second, JVZoo had been doing business for the better part of a year and Billy's company had still not launched. And third, the last email I received from this guy was a threat and a story about invading his dreams and plucking ideas out of his brain. Did he really think any type of partnership was an option?

He wrote, "Take as much time as you need to think things through with this proposition." As much as I wanted to, the guys convinced me not to respond.

Soon after, Billy and his partner, Jason, got their site launched. There seemed to be a small buzz in the industry about their new site. The reviews were mixed. Apparently, they were having issues with how their data was being displayed to vendors and affiliates.

Another conference was coming up. It was put together by Brian McCleod and Sam England. They told me Mike Lantz from Warrior Plus and Jason Edges were going to be there promoting their sites. McCleod asked if Zim and I would share the stage with them to answer questions about the affiliate marketing industry. We agreed.

It was always a pleasure seeing Mike Lantz. He was just a really sweet guy. The fact that we invaded his territory never made a difference in our friendship. We made jokes about being competitors, but it was all in good fun.

This conference was the first time I met Jason Edges. He seemed like a nice enough guy. He didn't have the hot head that his partner had, but he did seem a little nervous. Almost as if he felt out of place. Perhaps he was intimidated.

Despite the nastiness of his partner, I had no hard feelings towards Jason. However, I am a jokester and this didn't mean he wouldn't become the target of a bit of friendly hazing.

I was with Zim and Mike Lantz at the back of the conference room, standing by the entrance, when the announcement was made for all of us to come up on stage. Within a couple of seconds, Jason whizzed through the door and hopped up on stage. He sat down in one of the four seats set up for us. We all looked at each other and grinned. It was as if we all had the same thought. I said it out loud. "Let's let him sit there for a while." We all laughed.

The attendees were all in their seats, waiting for the presentation to begin. It was quiet. All eyes were on Jason. He was rapidly tapping his feet. The emcee was talking to somebody in the hallway. He was perfectly distracted. Several minutes went by and we still hadn't gone up on stage. It was just Jason, sitting by himself.

After a full eight minutes, the emcee, Brian McCleod, walked over to us, big smile on his face, and said, "You guys are assholes!" We all got a laugh out of it and then went up on stage.

It was a great question and answer session with the audience. Jason offered good advice and seemed well educated, but I think he was a bit taken aback at how much Mike Lantz and our team got along. We made jokes together, backed up each other's statements, and all around supported each other. I think Jason expected a battle for dominance. That was not the time, nor the place for marketing. It was about answering questions from the audience and being as helpful as possible.

A couple of months later, a new email from Billy arrived. He asked if we were interested in buying their affiliate network. He said that he had other projects he wanted to focus on and Jason is "just personally fed up".

His asking price was $80,000. Their site was still very much behind us in market share, but they were slowly gaining some momentum. It wasn't an entirely unreasonable thought to buy out a competitor that was gaining ground, so I responded by asking for details about the business. He said he would have a detailed prospectus in a few days.

I don't know if he was just testing my response, but the next email said he had changed his mind and decided to wait on selling the business.

Billy and Jason then launched an online chat forum, specifically for listing products. The idea was to duplicate the WSO section of the Warrior Forum. His next email was asking if we could make an agreement to encourage JVZoo members to list more items in his forum. I didn't respond.

Then, a few weeks later, came the final email from Billy. It started with, "I think you should have taken that 80k offer while it was on the table." "Now that we have our reports issues fixed we'll see what happens when we're running on all cylinders," he wrote. My favorite part was, "…and if you aren't worried about this then you're just an arrogant fucking prick who is going to be taken down one piece at a time."

What is wrong with some people? I think about the relationship I have with Mike Lantz and how I truly believe we each wish the best for each other, despite being competitors, and then I look at this guy. (Who treats people like this?) I later heard that Jason ended up selling his half of the company. I can only speculate as to what his motivation for selling was, but if I had to guess, it was to get as far away from his partner as possible.

Best of luck, Billy Runner.

Being in business is often like being in high school. You have to deal with competition, jealousy, and even sabotage. People grow up, but like in high school, you will have your groups of friends and the groups you try to avoid. My advice is to stick to hanging with people that inspire and encourage you. Avoid the naysayers and troublemakers - they will only drag you down. Leave the drama for the kids. Be competitive, but respect your competitors – you never know when they might turn into your ally, partner, or even beneficiary.

CHAPTER 23

THE NEW INTERNET

There was a time in human history when all you needed to do to get rich was come up with a good product and market it. That time wasn't all that long ago. In fact, this is how it was when I entered online marketing. It had been like that for hundreds, maybe even thousands of years, but things are a bit different now. Consumers are Internet savvy. They are no longer the sheep that listen to whatever advertisers tell them. They actually Google stuff before they buy it. This goes for everything from baby strollers to info products.

As somebody that sells information, it is important that I am seen as an authority figure. I'm sure many of you even Googled me before buying this book. What did you find? You must of seen something that convinced you I knew what I was talking about. Believe me, that was no accident.

These days, you have to take a proactive approach to how you want to be perceived by the public. Every business person knows that you can't please all of the customers all of the time. Unfortunately, the customers you don't please are the ones that are most vocal. On the Internet that can be very damaging. The last thing you want is for a person to Google your name and see only negative rants by unsatisfied customers. You must seed the Internet with positive stories and things that make you or your brand stand out as an authority in your industry.

It used to be that celebrities and politicians were the only ones under the microscope, but today, everybody is being judged online. Whether it's a consumer looking to see if your company is worthy of doing business with or even a potential employer vetting you for a job.

To borrow a line from the movie *"The Social Network"*, the Internet is written in ink. It's hard to erase what is there, so make sure that you don't play a part in your own online destruction. Instead, make it a part of your game plan to seed the Internet with positive things that make you look good.

When you make an achievement, glorify it with a factual press release. You may not get swarms of media attention, but people searching for your name will see it.

Create profiles in every social media site available to you. This includes LinkedIn and any site that has anything to do with your chosen field. Be aware that these sites will be used to vet you and your character, so think twice before posting a picture of you and the boys mooning cops at the local donut shop.

Participate in chat forum conversations, lending a helpful hand to people asking questions about your career field. Do not argue or try and one-up anybody. In other words, don't be asshole. Instead, be helpful and let people see that you know what you're talking about.

Start a blog. You can use one of the free sites at Blogger.com or WordPress.com, but the better choice is to register your own name as a dot com and install a version of WordPress. You can then write an article a week about your industry, showing the world you are an authority figure. If you're not the writer type, you can always outsource the articles for cheap. There are dozens of good writers that will research and craft an article for five bucks at Fiverr.com.

If you are looking to get hired, think about "Klout". Many employers are now looking at Klout scores. Klout is a service that measures your social networking reach. Sign up at Klout.com and link your FaceBook, Twitter, Google+, and LinkedIn accounts. Then, start getting active on those sites. Build a following by posting information and links to informative posts about your field or niche. The more interaction you get from others, the higher your Klout score gets.

Another way to look like an authority figure is by guest posting on major websites. Some of the most read sites on the planet allow people, like you, to submit articles on your area of expertise. The Yahoo Contributor Network is one. Yahoo gets millions of visitors, each day and their contributor network allows you to tap right into that. Forbes.com and even CNN have similar services. Joining these networks as a contributor can get your message to millions of readers and potential customers. These sites also rank well in the search engines. When people Google your name, it looks very good for them to see you aligned with these media giants. Most people won't even realize that anybody can contribute to these places. They will just think you are important enough to have an article on Forbes.com.

CHAPTER 24

REWARDS OF THE BUSINESS

JVZoo is a broker of information. I love that. Want to get some videos that teach you how to play guitar? JVZoo has them. Need to know how to cook faster meals? There's a course for that. Does your business need more visitors to its website? There's plenty of help in that area.

People have always had a burning desire to know more. Whether it's for personal or business gain, information is the one thing that will never go out of style. It's not a fad. It's not the flavor of the day. It's the one thing that people have sought after since the beginning of time and that is not going to change anytime soon. That is why I love being in the business of information. I made great money creating info products and brokering other people's info products. Find a topic people are curious about and provide the information they are looking for. It really is as simple as that – and you can do the exact same thing. You don't have to have be the founder of an enterprise sized business, like JVZoo, to become wealthy with info products. In fact, if JVZoo were to disappear tomorrow, I would be just fine. What would I do? Create and sell info products. Info products help people.

Building a business that makes you a lot of money is a great feeling. A better feeling is creating a business that makes you a lot of money and allows others to make money is even better.

In just three years, JVZoo is responsible for over $150,000,000 in sales generated by our members. While the news headlines are constantly reminding us about a failing economy and unemployment, my company has created a way for anybody to create their own income from home. It's a bit surreal, but certainly a rewarding feeling.

Somewhere along the way, I realized that helping people succeed is much more rewarding than any other field I have worked in. As JVZoo grows, it will continue helping people succeed by providing services that make things easy for them. Personally, I plan to continue sharing my knowledge through books, speaking appearances, and more info products.

It is a rewarding feeling to know that you've changed a life and it is very rewarding financially. To be a successful entrepreneur, only one of those rewards is needed, but to have them both just completes the package.

I'm not saying the business of helping people succeed is always savory. Like any industry, there are the good guys, the bad guys, and a bunch of idiots in between. The bad guys are the ones that just want to make a quick buck and have no regard for the results their customers get. The good guys are the ones that successfully build a real business around helping people. They are also the ones that make the most money. The idiots in between are the ones that preach that their business only exists to help other people make money. It's not genuine and it's a lie. The goal of any business is to make a profit. If you can do so while helping others, great, but if money was not the motivation for your business, then what kind of business coach would you be?

All I know is the more people I help, the more money I make and that can't be a bad thing, can it?

ABOUT THE AUTHOR

E. Brian Rose is a United States Air Force Combat Veteran, husband, father of two, Internet pioneer, public speaker, author, and all around nice guy. He is co-founder of JVZoo.com, one of the world's largest online affiliate networks.

"EBR", as he is known, travels the world teaching folks, just like you, how to find your inner celebrity and build a platform of raving fans and customers.

If you would like to book EBR for a speaking engagement or private coaching session, please contact his assistant at booking@ebrianrose.com.

CONNECT WITH
E. BRIAN ROSE

Web:
www.EBrianRose.com

FaceBook:
FaceBook.com/ebrianrose

Twitter:
@ebrianrose

Printed in the USA
CPSIA information can be obtained
at www.ICGtesting.com
JSHW081740120224
57198JS00009B/1036